THE BL
OF LIVING AGAIN
AFTER DYING

MW01613582

Minister Dr. LuEthel T. Green

Lu Ethel T. Green

University Press of America,® Inc.
Lanham · New York · Oxford

Copyright © 2002 by
University Press of America,® Inc.
4720 Boston Way
Lanham, Maryland 20706
UPA Acquisitions Department (301) 459-3366

12 Hid's Copse Rd.
Cumnor Hill, Oxford OX2 9JJ

Library of Congress Cataloging-in-Publication Data

Green, Lu Ethel T.
The blessed hope of living again after dying / Lu Ethel T. Green.
p. cm
Includes bibliographical references and index.
1. Future life—Christianity. 2. Death—Religious aspects—
Christianity. I. Title.

BT913 .G74 2002
236'.2—dc21   2002018749 CIP

ISBN 0-7618-2256-9 (pbk. : alk. paper)

Dedication

To the memory of my son
Eric Leon Green (1962-1985)

To my daughters
Leisa Meadows and Reisa Gayle Baynes

To my sons-in-law
Victor Meadows and Ronald Baynes

To my grandsons
Lawrence Meadows and Ronald Baynes, Jr.

and

To my granddaughters
Victoria Meadows, Erica Baynes & Miriam Meadows

CONTENTS

PART I
GOD THE FATHER GIVES LIFE

PART II
GOD THE SON GIVES ETERNAL LIFE

Part III
GOD THE HOLY SPIRIT GIVES COMFORT AND PEACE

Part IV
EARTH'S FINAL CHAPTER

PART V
A GLIMPSE OF HEAVEN

FOREWORD

The emotion most commonly associated with the notion of death is fear. As a rule, man fears what he cannot fathom, what he cannot explain, what he cannot see. What is indisputable is the fact that at some point we all must die. So death is a certainty. What is uncertain to many is what follows death. Do we simply cease to be? Do we find ourselves in an endless and dark void? While the world continues to wonder and debate about life after death, Christians enjoy a A blessed hope of living again after dying.

Of all the joys associated with new life in Christ is the promise of living again after dying, but not only that. For what makes Christian living so sweet is the promise that *if our earthly house of this tabernacle were dissolved, we have a building of God, an house not made with hands, eternal in the heavens@ (II Corinthians 5:1)*. Ours is the promise of everlasting life and eternal fellowship with our Heavenly Father. The Apostle Paul goes on to explain in II Corinthians 5:8 that to be absent from the body is to be present with the Lord. This is our blessed hope.

Without a doubt, the subject that this book broaches is very relevant. The message of encouragement that God has placed in Dr. LuEthel Green is a timely message to this generation. In this powerful work that illustrates God's mighty power to conquer death, Dr. Green sheds light on the promise available to every Christian. I am convinced that the principles illuminated in this book will be a blessing in the life of the reader.

Bishop Alfred A. Owens, Jr., D. Min
Senior Pastor of the Greater Mt. Calvary Holy Church
Washington, D.C.

ACKNOWLEDGMENTS

Grateful appreciation is extended to my Pastor, Bishop Alfred Owens, Jr., D. Min., for reading the manuscript; to my former Dean and Major Professor at Howard University, Dr. Charles Asbury, Ph.D., for advising me on the manuscript; and to Susan Peabody for preparing the camera-ready copy for publication.

PART I

GOD THE FATHER GIVES LIFE

INTRODUCTION

The Lord is my shepherd, I shall not want. He makes me to lie down in green pastures; he leads me beside the still waters. He restores my soul; he leads me in the paths of righteousness for his name sake. Yea, though I walk through the valley of the shadow of death, I will fear no evil; for thou art with me; thy rod and thy staff they comfort me. Thou prepares a table before me in the presence of mine enemies; thou anoints my head with oil; my cup runs over. Surely goodness and mercy shall follow me all the days of my life; and I will dwell in the house of the Lord forever (Psalm 23).

I believe that God commissioned me to write this book ten years after the death of my son. Initially, the book was completely about death, grief and mourning. I believed at that time that this was what God wanted me to do and so I wrote about my traumatic experience in the death of my son. It was on Easter Sunday morning in 1985, when my son died tragically in a motorcycle accident that "the valley of the shadow of death" significantly impacted and devastated my life. In my efforts to find meaning in what had happened to my son, my daughters and me, I searched the Scriptures and studied what had been written on death and mourning.

Whereas, I was quite familiar with death and mourning, my vocabulary was inherently inadequate to describe or explain in words the emptiness that I felt in the innermost parts of my being and the pain that I felt in my heart when I had to stand over the open casket of my oldest child and only son. I sincerely believe with every fiber of emotion that is in me that burying one's child is the most devastating and painful event that any parent will ever have to endure.

Although I wrote for two years, the book did not materialize as rapidly as I would have liked. But then, at the beginning of 1998, God added another dimension to my writing. God revealed to me that He did not want me to focus completely on death, He wanted me to write about life and eternal life, as well. He said that the theme of the book is "Love." God created life out of Love because God is Love. Then God sent His only Son into the world to redeem man. Because of His unconditional love for man-kind, God says to us: "For all of you who will accept my Son, I will place my Spirit in you and give you new life." You see, God's ultimate purpose is to transform man to the image of His Son. These revelations helped me to realize why I could not finish the book. I know now that I had the wrong focus. God told me that the message is not about me and my son, but it is about His Son, Jesus Christ who suffered, bled and died for us. Christ became a sacrifice for sin, and through His death, burial and resurrection, we have everlasting life. His name is Jesus and He is the Righteous Son of God; He is the Lily of the Valley, the Bright and Morning Star, and as I write this book, I am so happy to know that I am his child and we are his children.

Now, I found out that not only did I have the wrong focus, I also had the wrong purpose. You see my purpose, in the natural, had been to share my insights about how a mother can effectively work through the grieving process and achieve healing after the death of her child. But the message that God wants me to convey to each reader of this book goes a lot further than that. Whereas this may be appropriate to the healing of our psyche and it may help us to feel better temporarily; nonetheless, it does not give us the peace that lasts throughout all of eternity

Hence, the Spirit of God told me that the purpose of this book is not merely to educate people about the mysteries of life, death and eternal life. But rather, it is to bring salvation to the unsaved, so that they will have the blessed hope and glorious happiness of dying in the Lord. Because life in the physical state is merely a journey which is for a brief span of time. Death becomes that passageway through which we all must cross in order to shed the physical and to take on new spiritual bodies. Eternal life is achieved only through Jesus Christ. For after all is said and done, eternal life is that magnificent prize of being in the presence of God for all of eternity.

And finally, the Holy Spirit told me that the theme of God's love for us must be evident throughout the book. God commended His love for us; for while we were yet sinners, Christ died for us. God so loved the world that He gave His only begotten Son that whosoever believes in Him should not perish, but shall have everlasting life. And so, it seems to me that God would have me to say to each and every reader that we must love as God loved, and we must love and care as Jesus Christ our Saviour loved and cared. For God commended His love for us and Jesus Christ is that love. Because Christ loved us, He willingly died for our sins giving us the right to eternal life.

I am writing this book under the inspiration of the Holy Spirit. I believe that God instructed me to write on two different occasions. When I was obedient, the Holy Spirit gave me the words and Scriptures to write. This book is Scripturally based and to the extent feasible, I have quoted or cited relevant Scriptures, so that they may be read in context and in their entirety, as the reader chooses. All the glory and all the honor for the writing of this book belong to the Spirit of my Lord and my Savior, Jesus Christ.

In my opinion, the unique challenges of this book are as follows: First, to teach God's plan of salvation and to let people everywhere know what they must do in order to receive eternal life. Second, to bring about an awareness of the promises of God in the Scriptures, so that the saved can take hold of God through faith. And finally, to provide encouragement to all who are bereaved; as well as, to show that there should be a difference in the way that Christians live, die and mourn in contrast to Non-Christians. How should a Christian think about life, death and eternal life? What difference does faith in Christ make in the way we live, in the way that we contemplate our own death, as well as how we mourn the deaths of our loved ones? We generally like to avoid such questions because it forces us to confront our own mortality. I hope that this book will shed great insight on the perplexity of life, death and eternal life and will let the bereaved know that we have a special kind of hope in the promise of the Father of everlasting life in Christ Jesus. Furthermore, it is my fervent prayer that God's richest blessings will be bestowed on each reader; that you will come to know Jesus Christ in a very special way; and that you will be led to seek salvation with full cognizance of the truths regarding life, death and eternal life, Amen.

CHAPTER 1

WHO IS GOD THE FATHER?

Synposis

This chapter utilizes Biblical quotes in providing proofs of who God is. The first part of the chapter discusses the unity of the Trinity: Father, Son and Holy Spirit and cites specific scriptures that clearly express a Trinity in the Godhead. Explicit proofs of who God is are presented. The next part of the chapter is devoted to a description of God's Eternal being, His Sovereignty, His Majesty, and His Holiness. This chapter describes what God is like and depicts Him as follows: Spirit, Invisible, Righteous, Loving, Omnipotent, Omniscient, Omnipresent, and Immutable.

The middle of the chapter lists some of the more common Hebrew names for God and gives their English translation. Further, the chapter discusses and provides proofs that God the Father is the Creator of all things and illustrates the means by which the creation reveals the glory of God. Not only are the means by which God shows forth His Glory through various acts of creation demonstrated but it is also emphasized that God always works out of a purpose and a plan.

The final part of the first chapter discusses the mystery of life and various concepts and definitions of life are presented. Symbolic as well as physical descriptions of life are emphasized and relevant symbols and facts are cited.

If I were to ask you who God is? I am sure that most of the more common conceptions that people have of who God is, include beliefs such as "a supernatural power," "a powerful force in nature," "a power or force greater than man," "a power or force that controls the world and everything in it." Now, if I were to ask you, do you believe in God? Most of you would answer overwhelmingly, yes! But who is this God in whom you believe? Quite possibly this is the point at which we will find the greatest differences, particularly among Christians and Non-Christians.

Before we proceed further, we need to set the record straight. The God to whom this discourse refers is none other than the God of the Bible. First, the Bible tells us that He is the Father of Abraham, Isaac and Jacob (Gen.26:3; 28:13). God the Father is "Elohim," the one true God (Gen. 1:1) and the Father over the creation (Heb. 12:9; James 1:17). And this true God exists as a Trinity in unity: Father, Son and Holy Spirit. Moreover, the Godhead is one, the Glory equal and the Majesty co-eternal. The Father is the Fountain of the Deity, the first in order; the Son is the second manifestation, begotten of the Father from all eternity; and the Holy Spirit is the third manifestation, proceeding from the Father and the Son. And these three distinct manifestations of God are all one Glorious, Eternal, Immortal, Invisible, Only Wise, Almighty, and Incomprehensible God blessed forever. May I recommend to you the following Scriptures that clearly express a Trinity in the Godhead: "For there are three that bear record in heaven, the Father, the Word and the Holy Ghost: and these three are one" (I John 5:7); "...baptizing them in the name of the Father, and of the Son, and of the Holy Ghost" (Matt. 28:19); "And Jesus, when he was baptized, went up straightway out of the water: and, lo, the heavens were opened unto him, and he saw the spirit of God descending like a dove and lighting upon him: And lo a voice from heaven, saying, This is my beloved Son, in whom I am well pleased" (Matt. 3:16,17).

Second, God is the Father of our Lord and Savior Jesus Christ (Eph. 1:3). Hence, Christ prayed: Our Father which art in heaven (Matt.6:9); your heavenly Father knows that you have need of all these things (v. 32); and now, O Father, glorify thou me with the glory I had with thee before the world was (John 17:5). Moreover, Jesus prays for Himself: "Father, the hour is come; glorify thy Son, that thy Son also may glorify thee: As thou hast given him power over all flesh, that he should give eternal life to as many as thou hast given him" (John 17:1-2). In like manner, He prays for His people, His apostles, and for all the faithful; not only for those who believe now, but also for all believers to the end of the world (John 17:20). He prayed that they would be preserved in unity and truth in this world and glorified in heaven in the hereafter.

Third, God is the Father of all who believe in Jesus (John 1:12-13). Hence, God is the Creator of all of mankind, but only the Father of those who have accepted His Son. For this is life eternal, that they might know thee the only true God, and Jesus Christ, whom thou has sent (John 17:3). The Fatherhood of God was the key to the relationship of life for Jesus, and He gives that same relationship to us so that we can say as Christ said, "Abba, Father." In praying for his own, Jesus shows Himself to be a good Master of the family of believers in Christ. Before He leaves the earth, He commits them to the watchful eye and Council of God, who is able to keep them in every way.

Since God is not a created being, He is not subject to the limitations of time and because God is eternal, He antedates time. Moreover, the being of God is within Himself, wherein He decrees and takes counsel. Before anything came into being, God was, and is, and always will be. God is the Alpha and the Omega, the beginning and the ending, which is, and which was and which is to come (Rev. 1:8). The Lord God is the first and last who has called the generations from the beginning (Isa. 41:4).

Because God is sovereign and righteous, all of His acts are right. He is the Almighty God (Gen.17:1); He is the Lord of lords, and the King of kings (Rev. 17:14). He is The Wonderful Counsellor, The Mighty God, The Everlasting Father, The Prince of Peace (Is. 9:6). He is The Lord God, The Holy One, The Lord of Hosts (Is. 45:11, 13); The Great I Am (Exod. 3:14); and the King of Glory (Ps. 24:7-10).

God the Father is faithful and true, a merciful and gracious God, and He is a good God; who is kind, tender and longsuffering with men and women. And yes! He is A Great God! A Righteous God! And, A God of Justice and Mercy!

God has revealed Himself to man through the creation, through His Holy Spirit, through Jesus Christ His Son, and through the Bible which is the inerrant Word of God. In Old Testament Scriptures, names are ascribed to God which relate to His providential care of His people. Although there are many names in Scripture which are used to refer to God The Father in His provision and care of His people; in this context, I will limit our discussion by mentioning only a few Hebrew names which relate to God's providence, their English translation and Scriptural references:

1. El Berith, God Of The Covenant (Judges 9:46)
2. El-Elohe-Israel, God The God of Israel (Genesis 33:20)
3. Jehovah-Nissi, The Lord My Banner (Song 2:4; Ex.17:15)
4. Jehovah-Rhoi, The Lord My Shepherd (Psalm 23)
5. Jehovah-Jireh, The Lord My Provider (Genesis 22:14)
6. Jehovah-Rapha, The Lord My Healer (Exodus 15:26)
7. Jehovah-MeKaddesh, The Lord My Sanctifier (Leviticus 20:8)
8. Jehovah-Shalom, The Lord My Peace (Judges 6:24)
9. Jehovah-Tsidkenu, The Lord My Righteousness (II Corinthians 5:21)
10. Jehovah-Shammah, The Lord is There (Ezekiel 48:35)

We know that God the Father is the Creator of all things. Through faith we understand that the worlds were framed by the Word of God, so that things which are seen were not made of things that do appear (Heb. 11:3). The Word of God tells us that God created out of nothing, that is to say, of no pre-existent matter. And the very God of heaven who quickened the dead, called those things which were not as though they were (Rom. 4:17). The creatures were in the Logos (thoughts) of God before they took form. Hence, David proclaims: "My substance was not hid from thee, when I was made in secret, and curiously wrought in the lowest part of the earth. Thine eyes did see my substance, yet being unperfect; and in thine book all my members were written, which in continuance were fashioned, when as yet there was none of them. How precious are thy thoughts unto me, O God!" (Ps. 139:15-17). God willed things to be done and they were done. The Scriptures make explicit that God the Father is the maker of the heavens and earth (Gen. 1:1). He laid the foundations of the earth, that it should not be removed forever (Ps. 104:5). When we behold the beauty and orderliness in man and nature, we must stand in awe of God's wisdom in creating things with such beauty and excellency in character and spirit; and with such diversity and sophistication in form and function.

Of all the multitudes of wonders in God's creations, man-kind must especially stand in awe of the workmanship of his own physical body. The Psalmist proclaims: "I am fearfully and wonderfully made: marvellous are thy works" (Ps. 139:14); "O Lord, how manifold are thy works! In wisdom thou hast made them all, the earth is full of thy riches (Ps. 104:24). Since we know that God always works out of a purpose and a plan, we understand that the world is created for God and for God alone. It is totally for the sake of God's glory and honor as Creator that all things come to pass. Hence, God the Father has made all things for himself, even the wicked for the day of evil (Prov. 16:4). He made the earth by His own power, He established the world by His wisdom, and He stretched out the heavens by His discretion (Jer. 10:12).

The glory of the Lord shall endure for ever, the Lord shall rejoice in his works (Ps. 104:31). All of God's creations, especially men and angels, were created that they might give God the Father the glory and honor due His name, by acknowledging Him to be the one true God, the Creator of the heavens and the earth. The Psalmist David pro-claims: "O Lord our Lord, how excellent is thy name in all the earth! Who has set thy glory above the heavens" (Ps.8:1). "I will praise thee, O Lord, with my whole heart; I will show forth all thy marvellous works" (Ps. 9:1). "The heavens declare the glory of God; and the firm-ament shows his handiwork" (Ps.19:1). And the Apostle John writes: "Fear God and give glory to Him, worship Him that made heaven, and earth, and the sea, and the fountains of water" (Rev. 14:7).

The Creation Reveals the Glory of God

As a means of showing forth His glory God reveals Himself through various acts of creation. Although God can be observed in many phenomena in nature, this discussion will be limited to a brief focus on four means by which God unfolds or reveals Himself in the creation. First, the creation itself reveals that there is a God. Paul states: "the invisible things of him from the creation of the world are clearly seen, being understood by the things that are made, even his eternal Godhead" (Rom. 1:20). Further, the Prophet Isaiah presented many proofs from the creation, to show that there is a God, and to differentiate between the one true God and idols or false gods. An example of this can be observed in the following declaration: "Thus saith God the Lord, he that created the heavens, and stretched them out; he that spread forth the earth, and that which comes out of it; he that gives breath unto the people upon it, and spirit to them that walk therein. I am the Lord: that is my name: and my glory will I not give to another, neither my praise to graven images" (Isa. 42:5, 8). Likewise, the Prophet Jeremiah writes: "The Lord is the true God, he is the living God, an everlasting king: The gods that have not made the heavens and the earth, even they shall perish from the earth, and from under these heavens" (Jer.10:10-11).

Second, the eternity of God is revealed through the creation. God is eternal, before all time, without all beginning, and without end. Moreover, before the creation there could be no time, only God Himself, the Eternal Jehovah, who is not subject to the measure of time. Hence, God made all things, including time, as well. Therefore, the Psalmist writes a song of praise to God which declares that, Your years are throughout all generations, you laid the foundation of the earth, and the heavens are the work of your hands. They shall perish, but you shall endure, all of them shall wax old like a garment, and they shall be changed. But you are the same, and your years shall have no end (Ps. 102:24-27). And God's faithful Prophet Isaiah proclaims that God the Father has called the generations from the beginning saying: "I the Lord, the first, and with the last; I am he" (Isa. 41:4).

Third, the wisdom of God in creating the heavens and the earth and all things within is revealed by means of His orderly creation of many diverse things, and in giving each its own natural perfections. It is He that has established the earth, and it abides (Ps. 119:90). He stretches forth the heavens as a curtain; and He appoints the moon for seasons and even the sun knows its setting. The day is His and, also the night. He has established summer and winter; and by His appointment seed time and harvest time, cold and heat take their turns, Amen. Further, He sets bounds to the seas and adorns the earth with flowers trees and herbs. Therefore, we see God's wisdom being expressed in the orderly placement of all things: Heaven in the highest place, or atmosphere, decked with the sun, moon, stars and air. The earth was placed in the lowest place, flanked with waters, dry lands, mountains and vegetation. And God called the dry land earth, and the gathering together of the waters, He called the seas. And God said, let the earth bring forth grass, the herb yielding seed, and the fruit tree yielding fruit after his kind, and it was so (Gen. 1:8 -11).

Fourth, the goodness of God is revealed through the creation. God the Father is the sole and only cause of the creation. Evidence of God's goodness is seen in His creation of all things to give them being, perfection and beauty of being, and to give them specific being according to their own kind. God did not need to create in order to validate His own being. No! No! No! Every man and every women everywhere must understand that the creation is God's free act of love. In love God reached out and created the heavens, the earth, and everything within. Everywhere in nature we see God's goodness in the majesty of His creations. If we were to inquire into the reason that God created all things, and preserves, and provides for them, we would find the sole cause to be God's goodness. Moreover, the creation reveals God's goodness and everlasting love in creating things of which He had no need at all. Therefore, David proclaims the following: "Know ye that the Lord he is God: it is he that hath made us, and not we ourselves; we are his people, and the sheep of his pasture. Enter into his gates with thanksgiving, and into his courts with praise: be thankful unto him, and bless his name. For the Lord is good; his mercy is everlasting; and his truth endureth to all generations" (Ps.100:3- 5).

Many who don't know God may ask, what is God like? Although the characteristics of God are infinite and not fully comprehensible to our finite minds, I will list only a few of His frequently mentioned attributes. God is a Spirit: and they that worship him must worship him in spirit and in truth (John 4:24). He is pure Spirit, meaning, He has no material or bodily parts. God, the Father is invisible (Col. 1:15), Holy (Ps. 99:9), Righteous (Ps.129:4), Loving (I John 4:8), Good (Ps 100:5), Wise (I Tim. 1:17), and Caring (I Pet. 5:7).

God is Omniscient, meaning that He is infinite in intelligence, which is all-inclusive of the whole of knowledge. He knows everything that now is, all that has been, and all that ever is to be throughout all of time and eternity. Moreover, God is perfect in knowledge (Job 37:16), has infinite knowledge (Ps.147:5), and knows all of his works from the beginning of the world (Acts 15:18). He knows everything about man, including man's thoughts (Ps. 94:11), and even the number of hairs on man's head (Matt.10:30). The Prophet Isaiah asks: "Has thou not known? has thou not heard, that the everlasting God, the Lord, the Creator of the ends of the earth faints not, neither is weary? there is no searching of his understanding" (40:28). Hence an abundance of Scriptures substantiate that God alone has perfect knowledge, meaning perfect and complete knowledge of everything before it existed or occurred..

God is Omnipotent, meaning "all powerful" (Rev. 19:6); has power over men and nations (Dan. 4:17), and He has power over all creations (Ps. 33:6-9). God is Omnipresent, meaning "everywhere present and at the same time" (Jer. 23:24). God is Immutable, that is "He does not change" (Heb.6:17-18). And He does not vary or turn (James 1:17).

The Mystery of Life

Life is a mystery hidden in God and in spite of attempts at definition, none has been proposed which encompasses the totality of its majesty, complexity, massiveness, depth and breadth. Without a doubt, all of us must acknowledge that life is a definite entity, with its own unique qualities, characteristics and realities. Likewise, we must admit that life is universal and magnificent, consisting of complex, as well as simple phenomena. Hence, we observe life being defined in varying ways by physiologists, philosophers, and even theologians. Generally, the definitions or descriptions that these experts expound emanate either from a physical, a metaphysical, or a supernatural perspective, depending on their specific focus. Some Biblical authors have referred to life symbolically as, "fleeting," "transitory," "for a moment," as a "vapor," and as a "shadow." However, in order to fully understand the meaning of life, we must accept the spiritual truths which can only be supernaturally discerned, along with the physical realities that we can observe.

Most of us are familiar with life being described in terms of the physical functions that promote, maintain and sustain viability of the organism. For example, Webster's Dictionary defines life as: (1) the quality that distinguishes a vital and functional being from a dead body; (2) an organismic state characterized by capacity for metabolism, growth, reaction to stimuli, and reproduction; and (3) the sequence of physical and mental experiences that make up the existence of an individual. From a physiological point of view, we think of life as the maintenance of vital bodily functions for a span of time beginning at birth and ending at death. The accounts of the creation make clear that from the beginning, God the Father is the source of all life and He alone determines the bounds or limits on life. Therefore, God who is life, is the first cause, source and originator of everything. Hence, He is the living God, the living life, and the life of all that lives.

Chapter one of Genesis tells us that, "In the beginning God created the heavens and the earth" (v.1). "And the earth was without form, and void; and darkness was on the face of the deep. And the Spirit of God moved upon the face of the waters" (v. 2). David declares God's ownership of everything as follows: "Thine O Lord, is the greatness, and power, and glory, and the victory, and the majesty: for all that is in the heaven and in the earth is thine; thine is the kingdom, O Lord, and thou art exalted as head above all. Both riches and honor come of thee, and thou reigns over all; and in thine hand is power and might; and in thine hand it is to make great, and to give strength to all ... For all things come of thee, and of thine own have we given thee. For we are strangers before thee and our days on the earth are as a shadow, and there is none abiding." (I Chr.29:11-15).

God, the Father is the Absolute One and He is the source of all life and living matter. In Him is light and life (Ps 27:1). All things and beings derive their existence, power, light and life from God. Clearly, our heavenly Father is the source of all life and His Spirit is what gives life to all living. God's Spirit puts the rainbow in the sky, the blue and grey in the clouds, the twinkle in the stars, the fullness in the moon, the bright colors in the flowers, the green in grass and the sap in trees, the sunshine on a cloudy day, the sparkle in her eyes, and the bass in his voice. In other words, God's Spirit gives not only life, but He also gives beauty, love, joy, happiness and peace.

CHAPTER 2

GOD LOVES AND PROVIDES FOR HIS CREATIONS

Synopsis

This chapter further expounds on the belief that God is the Creator of all things, expresses the fact that man is God's greatest creation and discusses how man's purpose is revealed in the Word of God. The first part of chapter two defines providence and explains and gives examples of what is meant by God's providential care of His creations. Specific scriptures which attest to God's care and provision for the needs of mankind: body, soul and spirit are presented. God's plan of salvation for men and women and the reasons why Jesus came into the world are discussed extensively. The final part of the chapter discusses man's free will to accept or not accept God's plan of redemption. Specific emphasis is placed on the fact that the creation and a plan for redemption of man were not an afterthought, but were inherent in God's Sovereignty and Omniscience.

Both the creation and providence portray the nature and essence of God. Creation speaks to God's ability to cause things to be and providence refers to God's guidance and direction of all His creations toward the best possible ends. Moreover, the processes of creation and providence express the sovereignty of God. What this means is that God has absolute power, control, and authority over all that He has created. He alone is the Creator and Sustainer of all that exists. The Psalmist speaks of God's sovereignty in the following manner: "The earth is the Lord's, and the fullness thereof; the world and they that dwell therein. For He hath founded it upon the seas and established it upon the floods" (Ps. 24:1-2). God is our Heavenly Father and He loves and cares for all of His creations. By His power and might, God preserves the world that He has created. Hence as a testimony to God's Sovereignty, Nehemiah proclaims: "Thou, even thou, art Lord alone: Thou has made heaven, the heaven of heavens, with all their host, the earth, and all things that are therein, the seas, and all that is therein, and Thou preserves them all; and the host of heaven worships thee" (Neh.9:6). Similarly, David affirms God's preservation as follows: "O Lord, thou preserves man and beast. How excellent is Thy loving-kindness, O God!" (Ps.36:6b-7a). Thus, the Omniscient, Omnipotent Creator, the Author and Enforcer of all the laws of cause and effect can perform whatever He in His wisdom knows to be the best for His eternal purpose and plans in creating the world.   In addition to preserving His creations, God in His providential care, provides for the needs of all living matter. When God created the world, He created the seasons (Gen.1:14) and provided food for humans and animals (Gen.1:29-30). Moreover, the Psalmist testifies to God's provision of water, food, and refuge for man and beast (Ps.104) and to His satisfaction of the desire of every living thing (Ps. 145). Jesus said: "Take no thought for your life, what ye shall eat, or what ye shall drink; nor yet for your body, what ye shall put on. Is not the life more than meat, and the body more than raiment? Behold the fowls of the air: for they sow not, neither do they reap, nor gather into barns; yet your heavenly Father feeds them." (Matt.6:25-26). They that seek the Lord shall not want any good thing (Ps. 34:10).

Not only does God provide for the physical needs of human beings, but He also provides for their spiritual needs as well. John 3:16 and 17 make explicit that "God so loved the world that He gave His only begotten Son, that whosoever believes in Him should not perish, but have everlasting life. For God sent not his Son into the world to condemn the world; but that the world through him might be saved."

Jesus came into the world to "seek and save that which was lost" (Luke 19:10). Moreover, God is revealed to the world through Jesus Christ, His Son: "In the beginning was the Word and the Word was with God, and the Word was God. In him was life; and the life was the light of men. And the Word was made flesh, and dwelt among us (and we beheld his glory, the glory of the only begotten of the Father) full of grace and truth" (John 1:1, 4, 14). Likewise Jesus Himself, proclaims that "I am the way, the truth and the life" (John 14:6).

The Psalmist declares: "For ever, O Lord, thy word is settled in heaven. Thy faithfulness is unto all generations: thou hast established the earth, and it abideth" (Ps. 119:89, 90). Likewise, Scripture tells us that God makes special provisions for believers and "shall supply all your need according to His riches in glory by Christ Jesus" (Phil. 4:19). The Apostle John in testifying of God's provision declares: "Beloved, I wish above all things that thou may prosper and be in health, even as thy soul prospereth" (III John 1:2).

Moreover, the creation is not an afterthought nor is it arbitrary, but it is inherent in God's supreme power to create beings outside of Himself and to define and fulfill what is ultimately necessary to preserve, provide for and govern that creation. The free love of God creates; and by the very act of that creation, fashions the conditions in man and outside of man, including the real measure of his freedom, which controls his destiny.

God in Himself is Sovereign, Supreme, All-Sufficient, All-Loving and He alone freely takes counsel within Himself — God the Father — God the Son — God the Holy Spirit. The Eternal Father creates and preserves all things by His co-eternal wisdom, goodness, love and virtue. We must understand that the creation of life is a common action of the Holy Trinity. Thus, the Father is the commanding cause, the Son is the working cause, and the Holy Ghost is the finisher. God the Father creates by his sovereign will, the Son by His operation and work, and the Holy Ghost by giving life and motion. The beginning of the work is in the Father who creates all things by His wisdom and will and the Holy Ghost who nourishes, hatches, and hovers over the creatures to infuse life and motion in them. Although, God the Father is called the creator of heaven and earth, it does not exclude the Son and the Holy Spirit; it merely shows the order of the action and shows who has precedence. Moreover, as a Trinity, God freely creates according to His own good pleasure. In his Sovereignty, God can do whatever He wants, whenever He wants and however He wants. He bears witness and creates out of nothing but the power of His Word. He simply spoke life and the creatures came into being. However, where man is concerned, God framed man's body with His own hands and infused His breath into man's soul.

God, in His foreknowledge, knew all about man before the foundations of the world were laid. He knew that He would create man. He knew which physical, mental and emotional characteristics He would give man. He knew what needs man would have and He knew what to provide in order to preserve and sustain man. Likewise, He knew that man would sin and would require a plan of redemption. The Word of God tells us that God made man in His image and likeness (Gen.1:26). By image we mean the capacity to be morally responsible beings and by likeness, we mean spiritual nature or character. In other words, man was created with free will and with the potential to achieve a new spiritual nature through faith in Jesus Christ. Clearly, God's power to redeem presupposes His power to create. In other words, God knew everything that would happen before He created us. Therefore, the plan of salvation for man was developed by God before the foundations of the world were laid (Eph. 1:4). "For we are His workmanship, created in Christ Jesus unto good works, which God hath before ordained that we should walk in them" (Eph. 2:10). Hence, God the Father, in His Omniscience knew from the beginning who would exercise free will and choose His plan of redemption. Likewise, He knew who would exercise their free will and choose not to accept His plan of salvation. In other words God knew beforehand who would be saved and who would not. This gives believers assurance in knowing that our lives are enmeshed in God's sovereign will, supreme purpose and eternal plan. Before we were born, God designed our lives and patterns of living as individuals, in accordance with His will, pre-ordained purpose, and specific goals for each of us. As unique individuals, God has gifted each of us in specific areas. In other words, God has given each and every one of us a unique gift. Therefore, we should use our gifts and our bodies to glorify God in our own unique way and avoid the temptation to imitate others.

Man is God's Greatest Creation

David asks this question in Psalm 8:"What is man, that thou art mindful of him? and the son of man that thou visits him? For thou has made him a little lower than the angels, and has crowned him with glory and honor. Thou made him to have dominion over the works of thy hands; thou has put all things under his feet" (vv. 4-6). Job says it this way: "What is man, that thou should magnify him? and that thou should set thine heart upon him? And that thou should visit him every morning, and try him every moment?" (Job 7:17-18). Old Testament Scriptures reflect a greater focus on life in terms of man's physical existence, than is apparent in the New Testament. "And the Lord God formed man of the dust of the ground, and breathed into his nostrils the breath of life and man became a living soul" (Gen.2:7). Throughout Scripture, man has acknowledged his dependence on God for life. This is evident in the Psalmist's song to God, "For with you is the fountain of life" (Ps.36:9). In a later passage, he states, "Each man's life is but a breath" (Ps. 39:5). Other examples can be found in Job, who writes: "By his spirit he has garnished the heavens; his hand has formed the crooked serpent" (Job 26:13). In addition, Job proclaims, "All the while my breath is in me, and the spirit of God is in my nostrils" (27:3). Further, Job declares: "The spirit of God has made me, and the breath of the Almighty has given me life" (33:4). Furthermore, David proclaims in Psalm 139: "O Lord, thou has searched me, and known me" (v.1). "Where shall I go from thy spirit? or where shall I flee from thy presence" (v.7)? "I will praise thee; for I am fearfully and wonderfully made: marvelous are thy works; and that my soul knows right well" (v.14).

In the New Testament, the meaning of life is extended beyond mere physical existence to include a deep spiritual life that emanates from having an intimate relationship with the Lord, Jesus Christ. New Testament writers give special emphasis to the triumph and victory through Jesus which awaits those who accept Christ. As an example, in the Epistle to the Ephesians, Paul assured them that God has allowed us to know the secret of His purpose which is this: He purposed, in eternity past, according to His sovereign will that all of human history should be consummated in Christ; that everything that exists in heaven and on the earth should find perfection and fulfillment in Him. (Eph.1:9-10). The text of James 4 answers the question, What is your life? He stresses that we are but a mist that appears for a little while and then vanishes (v.14). He makes clear that life and death are in God's hand and occurs as He (God) wills (v.15). Since the beginning of the created world, being in the presence of God has been associated with light, life and completeness. While separation from God has been related to darkness, death and incompleteness.

That life itself is a mystery hidden in God and revealed to man when and how God chooses cannot be argued. The accounts that Moses wrote in Genesis about the creation were revealed to him by God. The Word of God makes clear that God the Creator and man the creature are not on the same level of being. Moreover, there is an infinite supreme distinction between God and man. The level of being from which God creates is an eternal fountain of supreme wisdom, dynamism and power. Why was man created? Why was I born? These are questions that have been pondered by many, both the lay and the learned. Moreover, it baffles our comprehension as to why God loves and cares for us, when some of us are so mean-spirited, so contrary, so hateful, and so hard-hearted. The answer lies in the fact that God knows our potential. God created us with the potential to honor, praise, obey and serve Him, by living a Christian life which will allow us to become all that God would have us to be. When God created us, He made us perfect in every way. Everything that each of us needs in order to become a wholly complete person in Christ is already on the inside. Whether or not we reach our potential is totally up to each of us. This means that we must change from a self-focus to a God-focus and begin to look at our existence on earth in a more spiritual light rather than in a purely physical one. Everything that we need to know about God's will and purpose for our lives is revealed in the Holy Bible, which is the Spirit-inspired Word of God.

Our Purpose is Revealed in the Word of God

When we search the Scriptures, we can find the answers to our deepest thoughts about our purpose. Throughout the Bible, we learn that God is supremely God, wholly Creator and absolutely Lord, and man is to remain totally submissive and obedient, offering up praise and worship to our Lord and our God. God is always Creator and Lord! He is not the substance of His creations; and there is no parity or continuum which binds Him to his work. The only continuity between God and His creations is the Word. The Word of God is not His being or His essence, rather, it is His commandment. God creates according to His Sovereign Decree and gives of himself to man solely as He chooses; consistent with His foreordained will and purpose. God decrees that His creations should affirm and continue His work. He decrees that all created things should live and procreate, that is, create further life. Moreover, the living differs from the dead in view of the fact that life is dynamic and death is static. Hence, the living can grow and create further life by reproducing its own kind; while the dead must rot and decay. God, in His Divine existence over his creations, wills to view his own actions in living development. He wills to see himself in his creations and He wills that his creations should honor him. We cannot divide our affections, therefore, our purpose in life must be to glorify our Lord and Saviour, Jesus Christ. God's ways are higher than man's ways and His thoughts are higher than man's thoughts. The Word of God tells us that all things work together for good in the lives of those who love God and who are called according to His purpose. Christians can be assured that in God's ultimate purpose, He is working out all things in our lives for His glory and for our good.

The Bible can be considered God's oracle to man. The Bible is without error because every word of the Bible is God breathed or inspired. The words of the Lord are pure words, as silver tried in a furnace of earth, purified seven times (Ps. 12:6). As for God, his way is perfect, the word of God is tried: He is a buckler to all who trust in Him (Ps. 18:30). Every word of God is pure: He is a shield unto them that put their trust in Him (Prov. 30:5). Therefore, the Bible testifies to the power and authority of God. We may surmise that God's plan from the beginning was to create a people who would choose to honor, praise and worship Him, even when they had other choices. Moreover, the purpose of the Bible is that we might see God's plan of redemption for us. Hence, the ultimate goal of God's Word is that we might be delivered from the penalty and judgment of sin.

The great theme of the Bible is Jesus Christ. The Old Testament prophesied of the coming of the Messiah, the New Testament pronounces that He is come and proclaims that He is coming again. The Hebrew's covenant was based on their relationship with God. Our relationship with God is based on our relationship with Jesus. You cannot get to God except through His Son, Jesus the Christ. By searching the Scriptures, we find out what our purpose in life is; we learn God's plan for our redemption; and the guidelines for our daily living are revealed to us. As Christians, we have a responsibility to know the Word of God. We must have the word hidden in our hearts that we might not sin against God. We must be submissive to the authority of the Word of God and we must obey His commandments totally and completely. In as much as God's purpose for our lives is that we honor and glorify Him, we likewise must have the same purpose in life. The Christian's great ambition should be to think God's thoughts after Him and then follow those thoughts. The Word of God says that through God we can cast down imaginations, and every high thing that exalts itself against the knowledge of God, and we can bring into captivity every thought to the obedience of God (II Cor.10:5). Therefore, the Bible contains all that we need to know in order to cleanse our thoughts and actions, to live righteously in this life and to receive eternal life in the life to come.

When God created man, He made man perfect in every way and intended for him to live forever in His presence. Man was created in the image of God (Gen.1:27) and since God is a Trinity, Father, Son and Holy Spirit, man was created a triune being consisting of body, soul and spirit. Man is the crowning work of God in creation and life itself is the most precious gift from God to man! Moreover, God has a perfect plan for each of us. God has a perfect plan for who we are and who we are to become; and He has a perfect plan about our lives and service to Him. But God does not force us to operate in his perfect plan; rather, He leaves us with the ability to choose. The purpose of our being here is to serve God and Him alone are we to serve. We are to seek after God with our whole heart, mind and soul. Because our spirits are the most perfect part of us, we must serve God out of perfect hearts and spirits. Only when we divide our attention are we no longer capable of serving Him with our whole heart.

CHAPTER 3

THE THREE-FOLD NATURE OF MAN

Synopsis

The chapter begins by exploring who man is, first from the Old Testament point of view and second from the perspective of the New Testament after the coming of Christ. This chapter depicts man as being created in the image of God, that is with a three-fold nature of man: body, soul, and spirit. The body is represented as being the center of world-consciousness, the soul as the means of self-consciousness, and the spirit of man as the center of God-consciousness.

The Bible is our reliable source of knowledge concerning the origin of man. We know that it is true because the Bible is God's Word. Hence, the Bible says that the man whom God created in His image, that is in freedom, was formed out of the dust of the ground (Gen. 2:7). Therefore, we know that man's origin is from the earth. Further, his bond with the earth belongs to his essential being. Moreover, the "earth is his mother"; he comes out of her womb. Man is created out of God's blessed ground from which his body is formed. Thus, the essential point of human existence is its bond with the dust of the ground or mother earth. Man has his existence on earth; he does not come to the earthly world from above, driven and enslaved by a cruel fate. In other words, man does not come from heaven; instead he comes out of the earth in which he slept and was dead. Man was merely a piece of earth, but he was called into being by God. And God breathed into his nostrils the breath of life and man became a living being. Since God breathes His Spirit into the body of man, and because this Spirit is life, it makes man alive. Hence, Old Testament Scripture reflect that when God turns away from man and takes away their breath, they die and return to the dust (Ps. 104:29). God creates other life through the power of His Word; however where man is concerned, He breathes into man the breath of life, He gives of His Spirit. Man as man does not live without God's Spirit. To live as man means to live as body in spirit. The body is the existence-form of the spirit, as the spirit is the existence-form of the body. This is an attribute that can only be said of man, for only in man do we know of body and spirit. Thus, the human body is distinguished from all other living organisms by being the existence form of God's Spirit on earth. God made man's body as a Temple for Himself to dwell in. Paul declares that the body is for the Lord and the Lord for the body (I Cor. 6:13). Our bodies are designed to be God's instruments, which He owns, in which He dwells, which He has redeemed, and which He will someday transfigure with glory.

In order to comprehend man's life or essential existence on earth, one must take into consideration the threefold nature of man. Man is composed of a body, soul and spirit. The body is the physical or visible structure that we see and is the means by which man maintains world-consciousness. The body houses the internal structures and the five senses of sight, smell, taste, hearing and touch. The second part of man, which is known as the soul, is the seat of the emotions, the affections or feelings. The soul is the means of self-consciousness. The spirit is the deepest and most perfect part of man and it is the part of man that knows. God gave man a spirit, an attribute which no other creature possesses. Only man has a perfect spirit and this is man's God-conscious part. The spirit is the seat of the faculties of faith, hope, worship, prayer, adoration , and reverence. Paul attests to the fact that man possesses a body, soul and spirit in the following statement: "And the very God of peace sanctify you wholly; and I pray God your whole spirit and soul and body be preserved blameless unto the coming of our Lord Jesus Christ" (I Thes.1:23). We know that the soul and spirit are not identical because they are divisible (Heb. 4:12), and that soul and spirit are sharply distinguished in the burial and resurrection of the body. It is sown a natural body (soul-body); and it is raised a spiritual body (I Cor. 15:44)

CHAPTER 4

THE BODY OF MAN

Synopsis

Chapter four presents the body of man as being a physical structure which is of a temporary nature. The body is not only the external frame which houses man's soul and spirit, but it is also the temple in which the Spirit of God resides. Further, the human body is depicted as being a magnificent, highly engineered, highly specialized, and highly organized machine. Specifically, this chapter defines and discusses some vital parts of the body which are essential for life. First, the brain, which is housed in the head is discussed, along with its functions of regulating bodily activities, receiving and responding to stimuli, and thinking ability. The five senses are discussed as a means of maintaining contact with the external environment. Other specialized structures which are discussed, along with their functional importance include the heart and blood vessels, the lungs, the digestive system, the elimination systems, various hormonal systems, and the reproductive system.

The "body" is the flesh or physical part of a person, whether alive or dead. It is the external frame or the physical temple in which the soul and spirit of the person reside. The body is a necessary component for a fully human existence. The physical substance of man's body is earth and water, and as such, it is only a temporary frame.

Water is the largest single constituent of the body and the universal medium in which the complex processes of life take place. Because water is so essential to the body; life itself depends upon a constant source of water and the proper regulation of water in the body. In addition to the anatomical features and the functional operations that keep a person alive, there are also the intangible traits that define who the person really is. Many people equate the body with who the person is, but human beings are a lot more than the physical structures that we see. To the contrary, each person is a unique individual with physical, mental, emotional and spiritual traits and characteristics which give the person individuality. We are all precious in God's sight and we are "fearfully and wonderfully made" (Ps.139:14). The beauty of the physical temple, as set forth by worldly standards, does not matter, what is important is what's on the inside. The wisdom and goodness of God is evident in the upright position and erect posture of the body of human beings, which is a privilege and advantage given to mankind over animals. Since men and women are the only beings in this world made to contemplate heaven, some theorists believe that it is appropriate that he should be postured to look upward toward heaven.

The human body is the most sophisticated and highly engineered structure that God has made. The magnificence of the human body is baffling to human understanding. When we ponder the hardness of the bones, the tenderness of the flesh and soft tissues, the toughness of the connective tissues and muscles, we can only conclude that these are the work of God's wisdom and power. Think about it — do you realize that even the beating of the pulse is not in man's power, but in God's? Furthermore, human life and all of it's mechanisms; the secrets of the frame; the powers of the soul; the ingenious operation of the brain, nerves, arteries, and veins; the systems for transporting blood, oxygen, fluids and nourishment throughout all parts of the body; the exact precision of the eyes; and a thousand things more secret and mysterious are all the workmanship of an Omnipotent and Omniscient God. The human body is perfectly and exactly shaped and framed; nothing lacking; nothing in excess; nothing beyond; and nothing short of due size. Hence, this precision and perfection in workmanship can only be attributed to the wisdom of a Sovereign God.

All of the parts or members are wisely placed in the body. God placed inside of man's body all of the vital parts that man would need in order to promote, sustain and maintain life. God did not create the world and then leave it to run by itself. We must clearly understand that, in the created world, nothing runs "by itself." Life and the innate potential to create life are the work of God. The fact that we are alive is almost beyond our control since most of our life-seeking activities are already built in and programmed by God. Thus, the human being is actually a self-regulating organism; and the fact that we are sensing, feeling and knowledgeable beings is in reality a part of God's purposeful sequence of life. Moreover, God has placed inside each of us everything that we need in order to exist under widely varying conditions and circumstances which otherwise would make life and living impossible. God has endowed every human being with everything that one needs in order to face life: every situation, every circumstance, every tragedy, every trial, every test, and every adverse happening. The human organism has the ability to move, to see, to speak, to hear, to respond to stimuli, to think, to reason, to make judgments, and to adapt to various environmental conditions. These abilities are all important aspects of the processes which are called life and are dependent upon the working together of every part of the body. Our bodies are vessels from God and should be used in ways that glorify God and fulfill His will and purpose in our lives.

Every part of the human body is highly engineered, highly specialized, and highly organized. Hence, the physical body is made up of a myriad of highly diversified structures. The human body is composed of numerous cells, which make up tissues; specialized tissues that join together to form organs; and specific organs which combine to form body systems. Further, there are networks and branches of nerves, blood vessels and lymphatics. In addition, each cell has its own specification and coding, each type of cell and each organ and system is specifically designed to perform a particular function. The importance of this specificity can be seen in the invariant actions of bodily cells and tissues in performing only the functions for which God has designed them to do. We can thank God for encoding our cells and designing our bodies in a manner that relieves us of the need to worry about our bodily systems getting crossed up or forgetting what they are supposed to do.

The Brain

The head is set in the highest place in the body and houses the brain which is the most highly specialized and complex organ of the body. The brain is the receiving and control center for all bodily functions; the primary seat of the mind (spirit); and the chief seat of the emotions or affections (soul). The brain joins with other specialized neuronal structures to form the nervous system. Hence, human beings interact with the internal and external environments through the nervous system, perceiving and responding to stimuli that continually impinge on them. The brain regulates all bodily functions and contains the intellect and other faculties which endow humans to think, feel, reason, and remember. All of the five senses are located in the brain, and all are placed in the head, except the sense of touch or feeling which is placed throughout the body.

The five senses are important members for maintaining contact with the external environment. The eyes, which are instruments of vision or sight, are the windows of the body. The eyes let in light and are important in allowing man to perceive and see the world. God has placed lids over the eyes for protection, and tears in the eyes for cleansing and as tokens of repentance. Next are the ears, which are like doors perceiving and taking in sounds, thereby allowing man to hear. The ears are important for grace because faith comes by hearing, and hearing by the word of God (Rom. 10:17). The ear that hears the reproof of life abides among the wise (Prov.15:31). Then there is the nose, which is for smelling. The sense of smell is vital in distinguishing between good or pleasant aromas and harmful or unpleasant odors. The tongue and palate are the senses of taste. This sense is important for nourishment and the preservation of life. The tongue is also for speech and, therefore, is an instrument for praising God. We are admonished to taste our words before we speak. Scripture teaches us that a soft answer turns away wrath, but grievous words stir up anger. For a wholesome tongue is a tree of life, but perverseness of the tongue is a breach of the spirit (Prov. 15:1, 4). Moreover, we must heed well that death and life are in the power of the tongue (Prov. 18:21). In reference to hearing and taste, Job asks, "Doth not the ear try words? and the mouth taste his meat?" (Job 12:11). Man has two ears and one tongue to teach him to be swift to hear and slow to speak (James 1:19). The last sense is that of touch or feeling, which is placed in nerve endings under the skin of the body and is very important for protection from environmental hazards. Touch receptors throughout the body detect sensations of pressure, heat, cold and pain and cause the body to respond by withdrawing from noxious substances.

The Heart And Blood Vessels

God placed inside of man many other specialized structures which are all equally important for life. As physical structures, the heart and blood vessels are vital in the circulation of blood for oxygenation and nourishment of every cell and tissue of the body. Without proper oxygenated blood, the tissues that make up virtually every structure of the body will rapidly die. This is true of the heart as well, which must also receive its supply of oxygen and nutrients in order to survive. The heart may rightly be referred to as the fountain and dispenser of life. Likewise, the blood and bodily fluids are absolutely vital and essential for life. The Word of God tells us that the life of the body is in the blood (Lev.17:11). Without blood in our arteries and veins we could not live. God has given all of mankind one blood, to dwell on the face of the earth, and He has determined the times and bounds of their habitation. For in Him we live and move and have our being (Acts 17:26, 28). In natural generation, the heart is the first to be formed and in spiritual regeneration, the heart is the first to be reformed.

The Lungs

The lungs are located in a protective chest cavity, surrounded by a protective membrane and a bony structure, known as the rib cage. The lungs are in close proximity to the heart and together they perform a reciprocal function of oxygenation and circulation of blood. The lungs and windpipe are so vital in breathing that many consider our breath to be our very life.

Other Specialized Body Members

God has strategically placed inside of man many other specialized structures which are vital to life. Man has kidneys for the making of urine; a liver for metabolism and the breakdown of toxic substances; hormonal glands for powering and regulation of certain bodily functions; mouth, esophagus, stomach and intestines for digestion and elimination; genital organs for reproduction; muscles, cartilage and bones for mobility; and skin and hair for beauty and protection.

Many of the body members which are of eminent use occur in pairs. Some examples include two eyes, two ears, two nostrils, two hands, two feet, two breasts, two kidneys, and two ovaries. This arrangement reveals God's wisdom in bestowing some of our members in pairs for necessity, convenience, and security, in the event that the use of one is lost. Additionally, God has provided many means by which man can utilize those substances coming into the body which are necessary for life and means for evacuation from the body those things which are not needed, which might be harmful or which might cause disease. Some of the means by which the body evacuates itself include sneezing, coughing, vomiting, sweating, urinating, defecating, and so forth.

Finally, the great wisdom of the Divine Creator is displayed in that there is pleasure associated with the satisfaction of those desires which are necessary for the support and preservation of the individual, and for the continuation and propagation of the species. In contrast, the person experiences unpleasantness or pain when normal drives are neglected or abused. For example, there is pleasure associated with the satisfaction of biological drives and needs, such as is experienced in eating food, drinking water, breathing air, and in sexual gratification. By contrast, deprivation of normal drives can produce discomfort and even wasting of bodily tissues when the body is deprived of adequate food and fluids, such as is seen in starvation and dehydration. God has given us physical drives which should be controlled by us rather than allowing our desires and appetites to control us. As Christians, God empowers us to not be slaves of our instincts and drives, but to master them by maintaining control over our own bodies.

If we belong to God, we should not injure, abuse, neglect, destroy, or in any way degrade our bodies. Paul teaches that sin dishonors a person's body (Rom. 1:24) and that the body must die as a penalty for sin (Rom. 7:24). As pertains to sins of the body Paul admonishes believers to put to death the deeds of the body and live (Rom. 8:13). Hence, we are to present our bodies a living sacrifice, holy, and acceptable to God which is our reasonable service (Rom. 12:1).

Also in the natural things of life, God has given man free will. The choice as to how one uses the body is up to that person. In other words, we can choose to use our bodies in appropriate or inappropriate ways. Men and women can freely choose what they will eat or drink and what they will not eat or drink; in what they will say or not say; in how they will use or not use their bodies; in practicing abstinence, moderation, or abuse and in many other ways. Likewise in moral actions, man has the liberty of choosing or refusing to act in morally responsible ways. Thus, we can choose or refuse to exercise temperance, discipline, moderation, honesty, and truthfulness in our lives. The Word of God has a great deal to say about how we should use our bodies to fulfill His plan for us and for us to honor His name. Our bodies are gifts from God, to be kept pure and in sanctification. "What? know ye not that your body is the temple of the Holy Ghost which is in you, which ye have of God, and ye are not your own?" (Rom.6:19).

We can say emphatically that the human body and its engineering by God is the most perfect example of organizational structure, form following function and division of labor. We know that this is true because you never see any part of the human body attempting to perform a function for which it is not designed. For example, the kidneys do not try to pump blood, the lungs do not try to make urine, and the heart does not try to breathe. The reason this is true is because, as stated earlier, each cell is coded and specifically designed to perform a particular function and this is what it will do. Hence we know that God is not the author of confusion, but of peace (I Cor. 14:33). Therefore, all things whatsoever are to be done decently and in order (I Cor. 14:40).

Again, I reiterate our previous statement that the creation of man is a part of God's divine will, purpose and plan. Therefore, Paul emphasizes the need for unity in the human body and the importance of the interdependence of its members (I Cor.12:12). In view of the fact that every part is necessary, the health or illness of one part affects every other part. Moreover, Paul portrays this relationship as follows: "For the body is not one member, but many. If the foot shall say, Because I am not the hand, I am not of the body; is it therefore not of the body? And if the ear shall say, Because I am not the eye, I am not of the body; is it therefore not of the body? If the whole body were an eye, where were the hearing? If the whole were hearing, where were the smelling? But now has God set the members every one of them in the body, as it has pleased him. And if they were all one member, where were the body? But now are they many members, yet but one body. And the eye cannot say unto the hand, I have no need of thee: nor again the head to the feet, I have no need of you. But God has tempered the body together, having given more abundant honor to that part which lacked: That there should be no schism in the body; but that the members should have the same care one for another. And whether one member suffer, all the members suffer with it; or one member be honoured, all the members rejoice with it" (I Cor.12:14-21, 24-26).

CHAPTER 5

THE SOUL OF MAN

Synopsis

This chapter defines and explains the nature of the soul of man. The soul is represented as the inner life of the person, the seat of the emotions, affections of the heart and contrary affections. The specific emotions and contrary emotions which are discussed in this chapter include the following: (1) love and hate, (2) joy and sorrow, (3) hope and fear, (4) courage and despair, (5) happy and sad, and (6) peace and anger.

The creation of man's soul is briefly laid out in Genesis 2:7:"And the Lord God formed man of the dust of the ground, and breathed into his nostrils the breath of life; and man became a living soul." This statement lets us know that although man's body was taken from the dust, his soul was given to him by God. Moreover the soul of man is made alive by means of a spiritual substance infused into the body by God. Hence, the spirit of man which is of a higher nature, being created of God the Father of Spirits, goes upward and is presented before the Lord in judgment after its departure from the body. The body cannot subsist without the soul and when the spirit is taken from the soul, the body perishes and decays. "Then shall the dust return to the earth as it was: and the spirit shall return unto God who gave it" (Eccl. 12:7). Therefore, when the body dies, the spirit remains alive and goes back to God. The spirit of the saved goes into eternal life and the spirit of the unsaved goes into everlasting punishment.

The "soul" refers to the inner life of a person, the seat of the emotions, and the center of human personality. The commonly accepted usage of the word "soul" refers to life in the physical body. Frequently considered faculties of the soul include what is referred to in Scripture as affections of the heart. The anatomical structures that are most often attributed with housing the soul include the brain, the heart, and the bowels or gut (which includes the intestines). Functionally, the soul is the seat of self-consciousness, or we may say that it is the affective aspect of the person's consciousness involving feelings and sensibilities. Moreover, the soul contains a psychic (mind) aspect which is the seat of strong emotions or feelings and a physiological (physical) aspect which prepares the body for immediate vigorous action, as is seen in the outpouring of adrenalin in the flight or fight response.

The soul and heart are often used synonymously in the Scriptures. Thus, emotions of the soul and affections of the heart refer to essentially the same phenomena. For instance, Proverbs 15:13 and 15 state that a merry heart makes a cheerful countenance, but sorrow breaks the spirit. He that is of a merry heart is continually happy. Hence, a merry heart is like medicine, but a broken spirit dries the bones (Prov.17:22). Within the heart or soul of man are contrary affections or emotions that may be experienced in response to various stimuli impinging on the individual. One such emotion is love, which is an affection of the soul uniting itself to something apprehended as good or seemingly good (I Peter 1:22). Contrary to love is hate, which is a strong affection related to the perception of something as being bad or harmful (Psalm 105:25).

Another emotion is joy, which is evoked by a feeling of well-being, enjoyment, success or by a feeling that one's desires will be met (Eccl. 2:10). The opposite of joy is sorrow, which is a state of mental distress or extreme sadness, usually associated with the loss of something loved (John 16:6). Sorrow is a very strong emotion, which was undoubtedly given to human beings because God foresaw a world of sorrow and woe.

Then, there is hope, which is an affection of the heart in which there is a longing or expectation of fulfillment of a good desire or the avoidance of something bad or evil (Psalm 39:7). Hope refers not only to the act of hoping (Rom. 4:18; I Cor. 9:10), but also to the thing hoped for (Col. 1:5; I Pet. 1:3). Contrary to hope is fear, which is an unpleasant often strong emotion caused by the anticipation of danger or extreme anxiety related to the loss of something good (Mat. 10:28). Fear may be directed to God or to mankind, and it may be either healthy or harmful. A healthy fear is reverence or respect. Hence, the Word of God teaches us that "the fear of God is the beginning of knowledge" (Prov. 1:7) and also "the beginning of wisdom" (Prov. 9:10).

Courage is an emotion that implies soundness of mind and will in the face of difficulties or danger (Amos 2:16). For the believer, courage is derived from a reliance on the presence and power of God in their lives and a commitment to stand firm on His promises. The opposite of courage is despair, which is a feeling of hopelessness and helplessness in a situation (II Cor. 4:8). In contrast to courage, despair arises out of a lack of confidence in the power and promises of God.

The next two affections of the heart that I will discuss are happy and sad. These are commonly experienced emotions and usually have no adverse effects, as long as the feelings are not extreme. Happy is an emotion felt in response to a state of enjoyment, contentment, or well-being (Job 5:17). The Scriptures declare that happy is he who trusts in the Lord (Prov. 16:20), and happy is he that keeps the law (Prov. 29:18). On the other hand, sad is a strong and depressing emotion felt in response to a state of grief or extreme unhappiness (I Sam. 1:18; Ezek. 13:22). Extreme sadness, particularly as related to grief, is characterized by a downcast countenance and a dull, somber, some-what ashen complexion. Pertaining to the countenance of a grieving person, Hannah went her way, and did eat, and her countenance was no more sad (I Sam. 1:18). Likewise, Nehemiah writes: "Why is thy countenance sad, seeing thou art not sick? this is nothing else but sorrow of the heart" (Neh. 2:2). The relevance of the countenance to sadness is mentioned by Jesus, who cautioned believer's against being as hypocrites, of a sad countenance when they pray (Matt. 6:16).

There are two additional emotional states which are relevant to our discussion and which in my opinion can have either a restoring or devastating influence on the individual in crisis. The first is peace which is an emotional state characterized by tranquility, calmness, and quietness of spirit (Col. 3:15; Rom. 5:1). The Old Testament meaning of peace was completeness, soundness, and well-being of the total person. Peace sometimes had a physical meaning, suggesting security (Ps. 4:8), contentment (Isa. 26:3), prosperity (Ps. 122:6-7), and the absence of war (I Sam. 7:14). In the New Testament, peace refers to the inner tranquility and contentment, felt by believers whose trust, faith and hope is in God through Jesus Christ. The peace that Jesus spoke about was a combination of hope, trust, and soundness of mind and soul, brought about by a reconciliation with God. Jesus Himself proclaimed this peace in His Sermon on The Mount (Matt. 5:9), and He also taught about this kind of peace at the Lord's Supper, shortly before His death (John 14:27). It is from the writings of the Apostle Paul that we learn that true peace and spiritual blessedness is a direct result of faith in Christ (Rom. 5:1). The contrary emotional state to peace is anger, or turmoil, which is an intense emotional state induced by displeasure or grief; the intensity of the emotional reaction can range from slight displeasure, to rage, to fury, to indignation, or even wrath. Anger is a special kind of bitterness of the heart that troubles and defiles the person (Heb. 12:15).

This short discourse on the emotions is intended to acquaint you, the reader, with the significance of the soul in confronting and recovering from crises in one's life. The important thing to remember about the "soul" is that our responses are based on our feelings which are influenced by our genetic make-up, past experiences and perceptions of what has happened or may happen. Hence, there may be one response as the result of a perception of something as good or pleasant and a different reaction when something is perceived as bad or unpleasant. In terms of one's psychological reaction, the amount of energy expended or the strength of the person's reaction is dependent on the degree of perceived threat to one's sense of self. Since man is a product of his hereditary traits and environment, the emotions emitted in specific situations and the intensity of the emotional reactions are individualized and will vary from one person to another.

Similarly, a person's reaction may vary from one time to another and from situation to situation.

Particularly in the Old Testament, feeling God's presence was equated with life and life was associated with the breath of life which is vested in man's soul. For example, Genesis 35:18 makes a literal reference to the soul leaving the body of a dying person. Nonetheless, there are numerous figurative examples that equate not feeling God's presence, with death, being alone and in darkness. In Psalm 42, David acknowledges that his soul cannot exist without the presence of God and he writes: "My soul thirsteth for God, for the living God: when shall I come and appear before God" (v.. 2a)? "Why art thou cast down, O my soul? And why art thou disquieted in me" (v. 5a)? "For with thee is the fountain of life: in thy light shall we see light" (Ps. 36:9). An example in the New Testament that depicts the use of the word "soul" to refer to "life" is as follows: Jesus taught "For whosoever will save his life shall lose it; but whosoever shall lose his life for my sake and the gospel's, the same shall save it. For what shall it profit a man, if he shall gain the whole world, and lose his own soul. Or what shall a man give in exchange for his soul? (Mark 8:35-37).

The essential point that I am stressing is that the distinction between the heart of man and the soul of man are not clear-cut. Thusly, there are various passages of Scripture which refer to the "soul" and the "heart" interchangeably. Particularly in the Psalms, there are references that suggest the heart is used when strong emotions or feelings are expressed. The following are a few examples: (1) "The Lord is my strength and my shield; my heart trusted in him, and I am helped: therefore my heart greatly rejoices" (Ps.28:7). (2) "Be glad in the Lord, and rejoice, ye righteous: and shout for joy, all ye that are upright in heart" (Ps.32:11). (3) "Our soul waits for the Lord: he is our help and our shield. For our heart shall rejoice in him, because we have trusted in his holy name" (Ps.33:20,21). "Create in me a clean heart" (Ps. 51:10). Other expressions include Hebrews 10:22, where Paul writes: "Let us draw near with a true heart in full assurance of faith, having our hearts sprinkled from an evil conscience and our bodies washed with pure water." In a similar context, Paul states in Ephesians 4:18:"Having the understanding darkened, being alienated from the life of God through the ignorance that is in them, because of the blindness of their heart."

CHAPTER 6

THE SPIRIT OF MAN

Synopsis

Chapter six is devoted to a discussion and elaboration on the spirit of man. The mind, will, conscience and the regenerated spirit of man are specifically defined and explained. Additionally, the various supernatural means by which God communicates with Christians are explained. This discourse includes discussions of mental images, trances, angelic visitations, and communion with God through prayer.

The "spirit" which is the deepest part of man contains the breath (spirit) of life. The spirit is the part of man that knows and which resides in the mind. The mind is the site of man's understanding, will, intellect, memory, and his capacity to think, reason, judge and be regenerated or reborn. The faculty of understanding guides man and is the means by which human beings become acquainted with God his Maker. God is a Spirit and cannot be discerned by any bodily senses, but by His Spirit. In the New Testament, the mind is clearly thought of as either good or evil. As Pertaining to evil, the mind may be "blinded" (2 Cor. 4:4); "corrupt" (2 Tim. 3:8), and "reprobate" (Rom. 1:28). In reference to good, the mind may be sound (II Tim. 1:7), willing (I Chr. 28:9), renewed (Rom. 12:2) and pure (2 Pet. 3:1). The will is another faculty of the spirit by which humans are able to freely make choices regarding good and evil. Hence, man was created with free-will, which is a faculty of the mind whereby one may willingly choose or refuse to do what his understanding deems to be good or evil. God does not compel man's will, but by rebirth and sanctification, man willingly chooses to embrace the will of God in his life.

The conscience is a person's inner awareness of conforming to the will of God or departing from it, resulting either in a sense of approval or condemnation. Thus this faculty of the spirit judges one's actions to be either good or bad. When we get saved, we get a conscience thereby opening the channel whereby the Holy Spirit can become partners with our thoughts and behavior. The Holy Spirit ignites the conscience and based on one's understanding and will, the conscience judges the action as being right or wrong. The conscience is that inner voice that tells you when you are doing wrong. Moreover, the conscience should bring about a change in the behavior, so as to bring the conduct under subjection to the conscience. In order to avoid sin in our lives, the conscience and conduct must work together. In other words, you cannot think it is wrong and still do it, nor can you think it is right to do and not do it. The conscience and the conduct must reflect who you as a person really are. Therefore to him that knows to do good, and does not do it, to him it is sin (James 4:17).

Within the regenerated spirit (or mind) of man abides the capacity for communication, communion, fellowship and intimate relationships with God through Jesus Christ. Communication with God involves not only our talking to God, but His talking to us as well. The most important means by which God speaks to us and reveals Himself to us is through His Word. The Bible is the Spirit inspired Word of God. Before God's Word fails heaven and earth shall pass away (Ps. 138:2). God places His Word above His own name, because God's Word is settled in heaven (Ps. 119:89). The purpose of the Bible is that we might see God's mercy, grace and plan of redemption for us. Again, I reiterate that the great theme of the Bible is Jesus Christ and the message is God's plan of redemption for sinners (Eph. 2:5, 6). God's will for His Word is: " it shall not return unto me void, but it shall accomplish that which I please, and it shall prosper in the thing whereto I sent it" (Isa. 55:11).

There are various supernatural means by which God communicates with Christians. A prerequisite to having God speak to us is to listen in silence. "Be still, and know that I am God" (Ps. 46:10). In times of troubles, God will always show up and communicate with the saints when they follow His admonition to keep silent. One type of supernatural encounter involves God putting thoughts in our minds. God deals with the mind because that's where the spirit is. Sometimes He gives us spiritual mental images or puts pictures, thoughts, and impressions in our heads; that is to say He speaks to us in visions and dreams. Visions and dreams provide instances in which God gives us supernatural insight, or awareness, and reveals messages to us. The difference between a dream and a vision is that dreams occur only during sleep, while visions can occur when a person is awake.

Another means by which God communicates with the saints is by means of trances. Trances involve mental pictures which are outside of the ordinary, and through which God communicates His will and purpose to us. Essentially, being in a trance involves being taken out of one's normal state of mind and being placed in a spiritual realm whereby one is receptive to messages from God. Some examples of revelatory trances recorded in the Bible include Peter's trance while praying (Acts 10:10); Paul's conversion and trance (Acts 22:17); and John's experience of being "in the Spirit" (Rev. 1:10).

Another level of spiritual encounter is when we have an angelic visitation. Angels carry out the will and sovereign purpose of God, as the servants and messengers of God. God uses angels to communicate special messages to His people. Being able to come into God's presence, to commune and fellowship with Him, continues to be just as important today as it was before Christ came into the world.

Of the numerous ways that we can commune with God, the most effective way that we have to maintain fellowship and intimate relationship with God through Jesus Christ is through our prayers. Prayer is the necessary link to receiving God's blessings and power, and for the fulfillment of His promises (Luke 11:9-13; Acts 1:8; Acts 2:4). Prayer is calling on God (Ps. 17:6), crying unto the Lord (Ps. 3:4), lifting up one's soul unto God (Ps. 25:1), seeking the Lord (Isa. 55:6), coming boldly unto the throne of grace, that we may obtain mercy and grace in time of need (Heb. 4:16), and drawing near to God (Heb. 10:22). Through our prayers we make the Word of God active in our lives (Heb. 4:12). We know that God's Word will not return to

Him void, but it shall accomplish that which He pleases, and it will prosper in the thing for which He sent it. We know that God hears us because His ears are open to the believer's prayers (I Peter 3:12), because He instructs us to call unto him, and he will answer and show us great and mighty things (Jer. 33:3), and because the effectual fervent prayers of the righteous avails much (James 5:16).

The most important and best thing that can happen to a person is getting saved, or born again. Jesus made clear the necessity for regeneration or rebirth: "Jesus answered and said unto him, Verily, verily, I say unto thee, Except a man be born again, he cannot see the kingdom of God" (John 3:3). "Except a man be born of water and of the Spirit, he cannot enter into the kingdom of God" (John 3:5). "That which is born of the flesh is flesh; and that which is born of the Spirit is spirit" (John 3:6). It is important to know that God deals only with man's "spirit" and not his flesh, because the flesh is sinful and is merely a covering for the spirit. Regarding God's Spirit, Jesus said: "It is the spirit that quickens; the flesh profits nothing: the words that I speak unto you, they are spirit, and they are life" (John 6:63).

Once we become saved, a miraculous and marvelous change occurs on the inside. Regeneration is the spiritual change that takes place in the heart of man, by an act of God which changes man's sinful nature, enabling him to respond to God in faith. In other words, regeneration is the supernatural work of the Holy Spirit by which those who were dead in sin are made spiritually alive. When man is born again, Jesus imparts to him a new nature, which means that Christ is in the heart of all who accept Him. Re-birth involves being washed in the precious blood of the Lamb, making Jesus the source of our spiritual awareness, and causing us to do good things for Him and His glory. Also, when we are saved, we get a conscience, thereby opening channels of communication for the Holy Spirit to come into our lives to help us live a righteous life. Scripture tells us that the believer is a new creation: "Therefore if any man be in Christ, he is a new creature: old things are passed away; behold, all things are become new" (II Cor. 5:17). And as the believer grows in Christ, he "should walk in the newness of life" (Rom. 6:4b).

PART II

GOD THE SON GIVES ETERNAL LIFE

CHAPTER 7

WHO IS GOD THE SON?

Synopsis

Chapter seven presents Biblical proofs of who Jesus Christ is. The first part of the chapter quotes scriptures which express the birth of the incarnate Christ and which attest to His attributes and characteristics of Deity. The middle of the chapter elucidates the reasons why Jesus Christ came into the world. Jesus the Christ is depicted as Savior, Advocator, Intercessor, and Mediator between God and man. The final part of the chapter defines and explains what God the Son is like: (1) Omnipotent, Omniscient, Omnipresent, and Immutable; (2) God's Divinity in a human body (dual nature); and (2) God's representative on earth.

God the Son is the second manifestation of the Holy Trinity. He is co-eternal and co-equal with God the Father and God the Holy Spirit in all attributes of deity. The Divine attributes which are God's very essence, and His glory which He will not give to any other, are given to Christ (Isa. 9:6). Christ is over all, God blessed forever — A-men' (Rom. 9:5). And He is to whom the angels celebrate "Holy, Holy, Holy, is the Lord of hosts: the whole earth is full of his glory" (Isa.6:3). God the Son was with the Father in eternity past and "he is before all things, and by him all things consist (Col. 1:17). He is the

King of kings, and Lord of lords (Rev. 19:16). In Him dwell all the fullness of the Godhead bodily (Col. 2:9), for He is the only Potentate, the King of kings, and Lord of lords (I Tim. 6:15). In whom is lodged all the treasures of wisdom, knowledge, holiness and all excellency (Isa. 11:1-5). His name shall be called Wonderful, Counsellor, the Mighty God, The Everlasting Father, The Prince of Peace (Isa. 9:6); of the increase of his government and peace there shall be no end (Isa. 6:7). He is the "I am" (John 8:58), "the way, the truth, and the life" (John 14:6); "holy" (Luke 1:35); "unchanging" (Heb. 13:8); "the God of Peace, the Good Shepherd" (John 10:14), "the Great Shepherd" (Heb. 13:20), "the Spiritual Rock" (I Cor. 10:4), "the Horn of Salvation" (Luke 1:69) and "the Only Just One" (Acts 7:52).

Jesus is the only begotten Son of God and has been present with God throughout all of eternity. The Apostle John declares Jesus to be the Word and writes: "In the beginning was the Word (Jesus), and the Word (Jesus) was with God, and the Word (Jesus) was God. Since the Word is God, He is equal to the Father (Phil. 2:6). Praise God, Jesus is the brightness of His glory and the express Image of His person (Heb.1:3). The name Jehovah is attributed to the pre-incarnate Christ in Ps. 83:18: "Thou whose name alone is Jehovah, art the most high over all the earth." All things were made by him and without him was not anything made that was made. In him was life; and the life was the light of men. Hence, it was the pre-incarnate Christ who appeared to Moses in a flame of fire out of a burning bush and said: "I am the God of thy father, the God of Abraham, the God of Isaac, the God of Jacob. And the Lord said, I have surely seen the affliction of my people which are in Egypt, and have heard their cry ... for I know their sorrows" (Exod. 3:6, 7).

No man has seen God at any time; nor is it in the power of flesh and blood to reveal this secret, but the only begotten Son, who is in the bosom of the Father has declared him. And the Word was made flesh, and dwelt among us, (and we beheld his glory, the glory as of the only begotten of the Father), full of grace and truth (John 1:14,18). Moreover, John declares that the Word existed not only "in the beginning" where He was "with God," but he actually "was God." And this Word became incarnate as Jesus the Christ, without relinquishing any part of His deity or His humanity. Hence the Bible portrays Christ as altogether God and altogether man. Jesus Himself declares: "I am the Alpha and Omega, the beginning and the ending, which is, and which was, and which is to come, the Almighty. I am He that lives, and was dead; and behold, I am alive for evermore, A-men; and have the keys of hell and of death (Rev. 1:8, 18). God the Son, whose personal name is Jesus (Jehovah) and whose title is Christ (Anointed One) is God in the flesh, that is the visible manifestation of the invisible God. Jesus the Christ is the only visible form of God and the only true light of the world.

There are numerous Scriptures that verify that Jesus is God and God is Jesus. When Christ was on the earth, He could forgive sins because He is God. For instance, Jesus said: "He that has seen me has seen the Father. Believe me that I am in the Father, and the Father in me" (John 14:10, 11). "For if ye believe not that I am he ye shall die in your sins. When ye have lifted up the Son of man, then shall ye know that I am he" (John 8:24, 28). Additionally, the Apostle Paul writes: "And without controversy great is the mystery of godliness: God was manifest in the flesh, justified in the Spirit, seen of angels, preached unto the Gentiles, believed on in the world, received up in glory" (I Tim. 3:16). The mystery of the incarnation is beyond the full comprehension of our finite minds, but the Word of God makes clear that Christ, who being in the form of God, made Himself of no reputation, and took upon Himself the form of a servant, and was made in the likeness of men; He humbled Himself, and became obedient unto death, even the death of the cross (Phil.2:6, 7, 8).

Jesus Christ is sent of God, sealed and authorized to give eternal life to believers. Moreover, a voice from heaven proclaimed at Jesus' inauguration into the Ministerial Office that "this is my beloved Son, in whom I am well pleased" (Mat. 3:17). And by a further Divine Testimony "a voice out of the cloud, which said, This is my beloved son, in whom I am well pleased; hear ye him" (Mat. 17:5). Therefore, by many signs and wonders, the Father has affirmed that Jesus is the Messiah; the Prince and Saviour, a light to enlighten the Gentiles and the Glory of His people Israel. Moreover, it pleased the Father that the Son should suffer bitter agony, bloody sweat, and an ignominious death that He may be declared mightily to be the Son of God, by His resurrection, ascension, and being seated at the right hand of God. The importance of this total process cannot be overemphasized; for if He had not been raised from the dead and ascended into heaven, He could not grant Eternal life to believers. Moreover, the Word of God tells us that if Christ had not been raised from death, believers would be yet in their sins (I Cor. 15:17). And if He had not ascended up into heaven, He could not appear for believers in the presence of God as our Advocator and Intercessor. Jesus said, "I am the resurrection and the life: he that believes in me, though he were dead, yet shall he live" (John 11:25). In Christ shall all be made alive (I Cor. 15:22).

In order to have a personal relationship with God, you must have a personal relationship with His Son, who is our life. Not only is He the Saviour of the world, but He is the only way to God and the only way to heaven. Because Christ is God, He makes clear that: "I am the way, the truth, and the life: no man comes to the Father, but by me" (John 14:6). Furthermore, Divine worship is due the Son. John 5:23 states: "That all men should honor the Son, even as they honor the Father. He that honors not the Son honors not the Father which hath sent him." Other Scriptures declare: "Let all the angels of God worship him" (Heb. 1:6). Moreover, "At the name of Jesus every knee should bow and every tongue should confess that Jesus Christ is Lord" (Phil. 2:10-11).

The requirement to get to know Jesus for oneself is so imperative that many Christians have formed personal expressions and symbolisms to describe what Jesus means to them individually. For examples, Jesus is called a bridge over troubled waters; a shelter in a storm; a battle axe and a mighty fortress in battle; a doctor in the sick room; a lawyer in the courtroom; a mother for the motherless; a father for the fatherless; food for the hungry; shelter for the homeless; a friend for the friendless; a comfort for the lonely; and a very present help in the time of trouble. Hence, the songwriter penned the following words: "Jesus is the Righteous Son of God, the Lily of the Valley, the Bright and Morning Star, and I am happy to know that I am His child." Another writer refers to Christ as "My Rock, Sword and Shield" and as "a Wheel in the middle of a Wheel."

Jesus, the Son of God is our Great High Priest (Heb. 4:14), who once and for all, by his own precious blood entered into the Holy Place, and obtained eternal redemption for sinners (Heb. 9:11, 12).

The Scriptures tell us that almost all things are by the law purged with blood; without shedding of blood there is no remission of sins (Heb. 9:22). Hence, the shed blood of Jesus Christ, God's Son, cleanses us from sin. For Christ has once suffered for sins, the just for the unjust, that He might bring us to God, being put to death in the flesh, but quickened by the Spirit (I Pet. 3:18). "Who his own self bare our sins in his body on the tree, that we being dead to sins, should live unto righteousness: *By whose stripes ye were healed*" (I Pet. 2:24). The blood of Jesus is viable and indestructible, it is still working today and it will never lose its power.

Jesus the Christ, is the Eternal Jehovah who tabernacled Himself in flesh and came into the world to die for man's sins. Christ lived a sinless life and He became sin for man. The Son of man came "to give his life a ransom for many" (Mat. 20:28). "For we have not an high priest which cannot be touched with the feelings of our infirmities; but in all points tempted like as we are, yet without sin" (Heb. 4:15). Jesus our High Priest is set on the right hand of the throne of the Majesty in Heaven (Heb. 8:1). Jesus the Christ is that triumphant, and glorious Champion, with dyed garments from Boz'-rah, having trod the winepress of His Fathers wrath alone, for sinners (Isa. 63:1-3). God the Son is the brightness of the Fathers Glory, and the express image of His person, who by Himself purged our sins, and then sat down at the right hand of God. And His Throne is forever and ever (Heb.1:3, 8). Jesus is our King who has the keys of hell and death (Rev. 1:18), who can bind and no man can loose, and loose and no man can bind.

Another important aspect of Christ's Kingly Power is to protect His people, and He sends His angels to uphold believers and protect them in all their ways (Ps. 91:11). Hence, when Christians face trials and troubles, He strengthens them by His Grace, and assists them with patience, until He gives them a way of escape. Moreover, the Apostle Paul writes: "There hath no temptation taken you but such as is common to man; but God is faithful, who will not suffer you to be tempted above that ye are able; but will with the temptation also make a way to escape, that ye may be able to bear it" (I Cor. 10:13)

Therefore, we are admonished to look unto Jesus who is the author and finisher of our faith; who for the joy that was set before Him endured the cross, despising the shame, and is set down at the right hand of God (Heb. 12:2). In addition, Jesus is that infallible Prophet, the way, the truth and life; to lead and instruct His people (John 14:6). In beauty, He is the Rose of Sharon and the Lily of the Valley, The Bright and Morning Star, the image of the invisible God and the Brightness of His Glory, and the express Image of his Person (Song 2:1; Rev. 22:16; Heb. 1:3). And He is to believers wisdom, righteousness, sanctification and redemption (I Cor. 1:30).

Jesus is our Intercessor, Advocator and Mediator between God and man. He is able to save them to the uttermost that come unto him, seeing He ever lives to make intercession for them (Heb. 7:25). Jesus Christ, the Righteous is our Advocate with the Father. And He is the propitiation for our sins: and not for our's only, but also for the sins of the whole world (I John 2:1, 2). For Christ has entered into Heaven itself, to appear in the presence of God for us (Heb. 9:24). He speaks to God for us and He speaks to us for God. He is the one Mediator between God and men, the man Christ Jesus; who gave Himself a ransom for all (I Tim. 2:5, 6). For He has blotted out our transgressions, and will not remember our sins (Isa. 43:25). Therefore, He has quickened those who were dead in sins, has forgiven our trespasses, blotted out the handwriting of ordinances that were against us, which were contrary to us, and took it out of the way, nailing it to his cross (Col. 3:13-14). Without a doubt, the resources of Christ in every realm of human existence are limitless; His power is infinite; and His grace is boundless.

Moreover, our Lord Jesus Christ is our Reconciler, putting us in right relationship with God. "For if, when we were enemies, we were reconciled to God by the death of his Son, much more, being reconciled, we shall be saved by his life" (Rom. 5:10). And God has reconciled us to Himself by Jesus Christ, for "God was in Christ, reconciling the world unto himself" (II Cor. 5:18, 19). Moreover, God is Christ and Christ is God and they are the same forevermore. Jesus said to Philip "He that has seen me has seen the Father; Believe thou not that I am in the Father, and the Father in me? the words that I speak unto you I speak not of myself: but the Father that dwells in me, he does the works. Believe me that I am in the Father, and the Father in me (John 14:9, 10, 11).

What is God the Son Like?

God the Son is the image of the invisible God (Col 2:2). He is the visible form of God and the only begotten Son of God (John 1:18). He is God's Divinity in a human body and therefore, has a dual nature: Divine and human. In his Divinity, He is God and will always be God. Moreover, in His Deity, He is Omnipotent, "all powerful" (Mat. 28:18); Omniscient, "all knowing" (John 16:30); Omnipresent, "everywhere present" (Mat. 18:20; 28:20); and Immutable, "never changes" (Heb. 6:17, 18). Likewise, He has power over nature (Col. 1:16-17); and Death (John 11:25-26; Rev.1:18); He knows our thoughts (Mat: 9:4; 12:25); He has the power to give rest (Mat. 11:28, 29); to heal (Mat. 10:8; Luke 4:18); to forgive sins (Luke 5:24); to cast out demons (Mat. 9:33, 34) and to raise his own body from the dead (Gal. 1:1). The Deity of Christ is characterized by Godliness, Goodness, Holiness, Righteousness, and Love. Greater love has no man than this, that a man lay down his life for his friends (John 15:13), "but God commends his love for us, in that while we were yet sinners, Christ died for us" (Rom. 5:8). We become partners to Christ's Divine nature when we accept Christ and are "born again." Peter wrote: "According as his divine power has given unto us all things that pertain unto life and godliness through the knowledge of him that has called us to glory and virtue. Whereby are given unto us exceeding great and precious promises: that by these ye might be partakers of the divine nature, having escaped the corruption which is in the world through lust" (II Pet. 1:3, 4).

Jesus is God's representative on earth and they shall call His name Emanuel which means God with us (Mat. 1:23). Jesus is the infleshment or touchable manifestation of the invisible God. In order to make the invisible God touchable, He had to take on an incarnated nature or human form. This means that God himself became a man; moreover, God and Jesus are in fact the same and at the end of time, Jesus will revert back to the source that spoke Him into existence in the first place. Jesus differed from an ordinary human in that He possessed the unlimited power, authority and character of God, and He was full of the presence of God. Jesus came for a two-fold purpose: (1) To make God visible, and (2) To reveal God's plan of redemption.

"Wherefore in all things it behooved him to be made like unto his brethren, that he might be a merciful and faithful high priest in things pertaining to God, to make reconciliation for the sins of the people" (Heb. 2:17). God the Son knew the consequences of man's sin and willingly came to earth in the form of humanity to pay that price (Phil. 2:6-8). Jesus said: "I lay down my life, that I might take it again. No man takes it from me, but I lay it down of myself. I have the power to lay it down, and I have the power to take it again" (John 10:17, 18).

As a man, Christ lived the most perfect life ever known. He was kind, gentle, sympathetic, tender and patient. Jesus loved people and worked miracles to feed the hungry, heal the sick and infirm, and to bind up the wounded of body and spirit. When Jesus' earthly ministry began, He went into the Synagogue and turned to the book of Isaiah, which He opened and read:

> *The spirit of the lord is upon me, because he hath anointed me to preach the gospel to the poor; he hath sent me to heal the brokenhearted, to preach deliverance to the captives, and recovering of sight to the blind, to set at liberty them that are bruised, to preach the acceptable year of the lord* (Luke 4:18, 19). Then He closed the book and said to them, "this day is this scripture fulfilled in your ears" (Luke 4:21).

Not only has Christ raised man from the miserable state of sin, but He has also raised human-kind to the highest estate of honor, glory, and eternal happiness, by making them heirs of eternal life, and joint heirs with Christ in Glory. For as many as received Him to them He gave the power to become the sons of God, even to them that believe on His name (John 1:12). And if children, then heirs; heirs of God and joint-heirs with Christ (Rom. 8:17). Hence, Jesus said: "And the glory which thou gave me I have given them; that they may be one, even as we are one" (John 17:22). "There is therefore now no condemnation to them which are in Christ Jesus, who walk not after the flesh, but after the Spirit. For whom he did foreknow, he also did predestinate to be conformed to the image of his Son, that he might be the firstborn among many brethren. Who shall lay anything to the charge of God's elect? It is God that justifies. It is Christ that died, yea rather, that is risen again, who is at the right hand of God, who also makes intercession for us" (Rom. 8:1, 29, 33, 34). Moreover, Jesus is that merciful High Priest, who has offered Himself once and for all, a sacrifice for sinners and who is able to save to the uttermost those who come to Him. For He is that only Potentate and Bountiful Prince, who rewards the faith and obedience of His people with Eternal glory.

The name of Jesus is important, because there is power in that name. Wherefore, God has highly exalted him, and given him a name that is above every name. And at the name of Jesus every knee should bow, of things in heaven, and things in earth, and things under the earth (Phil.2:10). Prayer is made unto Jesus and saints are admonished to call upon the name of Jesus (I Cor.1:2). And they stoned Stephen, calling upon God, and saying, Lord Jesus, receive my spirit (Acts 7:59). Hence, in Acts 4:12, the Apostle Peter declares: "Neither is there salvation in any other: for there is none other name under heaven given among men, whereby we must be saved." And the Apostle Paul writes: "For I am not ashamed of the gospel of Christ: for it is the power of God unto salvation to every one that believes" (Rom. 1:16). Essentially, all these Scriptures have one message, and that message is that Jesus is the only way that we can receive eternal life. In order to be saved, you must come to know Jesus for yourself. He is the only way to God and the only way to heaven.

CHAPTER 8

THE PROMISES OF GOD TO BELIEVERS

Synopsis

This chapter defines and discusses the unconditional and conditional promises of God. The promises of God to believers are categorized as "spiritual" and "temporal." Spiritual promises are expressed as being eternal (everlasting) and temporal promises are described as fleeting or temporary. The chapter elaborates on some of the spiritual blessings that Christians enjoy in this life on earth and in the life to come in heaven.

The final part of the chapter discusses specific promises of God in the following situations: (1) In mourning; (2) In trials and afflictions; and (3) When alone and forsaken.

✧ ✧ ✧ ✧

The first duty that men and women have in order to attain Eternal Life is to search the Scriptures for the Promises of God in Jesus Christ, and believe them. A promise is a pledge to perform or to grant a specific thing. In Scripture, God enters into what is called covenant relationships with His people. Some of God's promises to His people are unconditional and some are conditional. Therefore, what God has promised unconditionally, means that He alone will do all that is necessary to fulfill the promise. By contrast, conditional promises are kept by God depending on man's response to His Holy commands.

Every person must clearly understand that God did not have to promise anything to sinful people. Nonetheless, God made promises to those who accept His plan of salvation, indicating his Grace, Love, Mercy, and Faithfulness to those who belong to Christ. Moreover, Jesus teaches: "search the scriptures; for in them ye think ye have eternal life: and these are they that testify of me" (John 5:39). The promise of eternal life is offered to all who will believe and trust in Jesus Christ. Therefore, Christians should put their complete confidence and trust in the promises of God which are found in the Holy Scriptures.

The promises of Christ to believers can be categorized as either "Spiritual" or "Temporal." On the one hand, spiritual promises are non-material, pertain to the mind or spirit of man and have to do with our thoughts or beliefs about the Holy Trinity, Salvation, and Eternal Life. On the other hand, temporal promises pertain to the natural and relate to what God has promised Christians as we face the day-to-day life situations and conditions in our lives. There are distinct differences between that which is spiritual and that which is temporal. First, all things temporal or things of this life are temporary, subject to changes, are uncertain, and unstable; but things spiritual are eternal and permanent. Thus, spiritual promises are not seen and are eternal, while the temporal are seen and fleeting (II Cor. 4:18). Second, temporal things leave the person at the grave, and in this life; whereas, when this life is ended, the spiritual continues into eternity and the saved enter into eternal rest. Third, the pleasures of this life are imperfect and cannot make the person happy who has them. But the spiritual are eternal and perfect, and the Saints of God are happy in them.

Therefore, all the enjoyments of worldly pleasures fall short of the joy found in the eternal inheritance of the saints, which is in Jesus Christ and which leads to eternal life. Hence, when the natural life ends, the Saints of God are happy in their death, for then their spiritual life of blessed enjoyments begins. Therefore, the blessed hope and spiritual enjoyments promised to the saved are not seen or apprehended by the natural senses, but are spiritually discerned, and are eternal and forever. In His great Sermon on the Mount Jesus advises us not to seek treasures upon earth, but to seek treasure in heaven where moth and rust do not corrupt and where thieves do no break through and steal. For where your treasure is, there will your heart be also (Mat. 6:19 - 21).

Solomon, the preacher accounts all human things and all human days as continual sorrow, vanity and vexation of the spirit. For in much wisdom, there is much grief and in increased knowledge, there is increased sorrow. And there is nothing new under the sun (Eccl. 1:2, 9, 14 - 18). In terms of everyday living, we are all keenly aware of how precarious, unstable and uncertain life can be. In the process of adapting to situations and events in our lives, all of us have our good days and our bad days; but for the Christian, the good days generally outnumber the bad ones and we can say, "thank you Lord for what you've done for me." You see, as Christians, we have learned to lean and depend on Jesus to bring us through each and every one of life's circumstances.

Most of us can handle fairly well the minor upsets in our lives: The car that won't start; the toilet that backs up; the traffic jams in getting to and from work; the missed bus when you are already late; the runs in your stockings before an important engagement; the running out of bread and/or milk at breakfast time; the special dinner that you burned; and so forth. Oh! - but, every now and then, we face a catastrophic event in our lives that stops us in our tracks; that causes us to not want to go on; that causes us to not want to try anymore; and yes, that even causes us to not want to live! Think about it, have you ever received a bad report from the doctor? Have you ever lost your job? your house? Have you ever had a love one to die, when you had prayed and claimed their healing? Has your child died suddenly in an accident ? or maybe, after a long terminal illness? What about losing a limb, your eyesight, or becoming paralyzed? Have you ever lost all of your earthly possessions in a fire? And, Oh! the list goes on and on! Therefore, I will not attempt to list all the tragedies in life, because the list is too exhaustive. Suffice it to say that the severe tragedies and the catastrophes that we face in life are the ones that give us the most difficulty and they are the ones which negatively impact our well-being. Leaving us in need of assistance in the form of significant holistic support, preservation of the mind (spirit) and body, and protection and care of the emotions (soul).

First of all, let us focus our attention on three relevant "Spiritual Promises" which are stated as follows: (1) The Promise of a Redeemer (Gen.3:15); (2) The Promise of Grace and Spiritual blessings for God's elect (Rom. 8:28); (3) The Promise of Eternal Life and Salvation to all who believe in Jesus Christ (John 3:16).

In Genesis 3:15, we find the first Promise of God and the first direct prophecy of Jesus Christ in Scripture. The Redeemer of man had to be One who was not tainted by sin and who could fulfill the Holy demands of God perfectly. Moreover, God through the shed blood of Jesus Christ has shown His free pardon of all our transgressions and sins, by the full and complete act of oblivion which is entered in the records of heaven. "I, even I, am he that blots out thy transgressions for mine own sake, and will not remember thy sins (Isa. 43:25). Furthermore, "I have blotted out as a thick cloud, thy transgressions, and, as a cloud, thy sins return unto me; for I have redeemed thee" (Isa. 44:22). In speaking of Him who is to conquer Satan, God calls him the "seed of woman," which indicates that He had no earthly father. Therefore the Lord himself shall give you a sign; Behold, a virgin shall conceive, and bear a son and shall call his name Immanuel (Isa. 7:14), which means "God with us, or God is with us." Thus, God revealed in this marvelous prophecy that God Himself would enter the human realm through miraculous conception, and redeem man. In keeping with this Promise, the prophet Isaiah declares: "For unto us a child is born, unto us a son is given: and the government shall be upon his shoulder: and his name shall be called Wonderful, Counsellor, the mighty God, the everlasting Father, the Prince of Peace. Of the increase of his government and peace there shall be no end" (Isa. 9:6, 7).

The Promise in Genesis is the initiation of God's redemptive plan for man and His Promise to send a Redeemer into the world to save man from his sins. Literally, redemption is the process of buying back for a price. Jesus paid the price that was necessary to buy back our salvation: "Neither by the blood of goats and calves, but by his own blood he entered once into the holy place, having obtained eternal redemption for us. How much more shall the blood of Christ, who through the eternal Spirit offered himself without spot to God, purge your conscience from dead works to serve the living God" (Heb. 9:12, 14)? Hence, we should always remember the tremendous price of our redemption: "the precious blood of Christ" (I Pet.1:19; Eph. 1:7), which is also called an atoning sacrifice "a propitiation by his blood" (Rom. 3:25). We must always glorify God, give Him praise and rejoice in knowing that we have been made free from the power of sin (Rom. 6:18), and the fear of death (Heb. 2:14, 15). Yes, Christ gave Himself for us, that he might redeem us from all iniquity, and purify unto Himself a peculiar people, zealous of good works (Titus 2:14). For in Him, we have redemption through His blood, and the forgiveness of sins, according to the riches of His grace (Eph. 1:7). Moreover, if the Son shall make you free, you shall be free indeed (John 8:36).

The Promise of a Redeemer is an unconditional covenant, which was completely fulfilled in Jesus Christ. The aforementioned prophecy in Isaiah 7:14 foretells of God's promise to send one of the manifestations of the Godhead into the world as the Redeemer of humanity. "And all things are of God, who hath reconciled us to himself by Jesus Christ. To wit, that God was in Christ, reconciling the world unto himself, not imputing their trespasses unto them" (II Cor. 5:18, 19). This Promise reflects the free love of God in sending Christ as a ransom for the sinful estate of mankind. Jesus came into the world as promised in the Scriptures to save sinners by His death on the cross, according to the deliberate will and plan of God, to provide a way for sinners to obtain a right relationship with God and receive the gift of Eternal Life. For Christ has once suffered for sins, the just for the unjust, that he might bring us to God (I Peter 3:18). By means of the sacrifices of Christ, believer's are clothed with the righteousness of Christ and receive a new spiritual nature. For by one offering, Christ has perfected forever those who are sanctified (Heb.10:14). And today our risen Saviour promises every Christian that "because I live, ye shall live also" (John 14:19).

The second Spiritual Promise pertains to the Grace of God and the Spiritual Blessings that are bestowed on those who are called according to His purpose. When we speak of God's grace, we refer to the unmerited or unwarranted kindness and favor that God bestows on those who belong to Him. Likewise, to bless means to speak well of: or to declare, wish or bestow favor and goodness upon another. Grace is one of the major characteristics of God. God blesses us, not because we are deserving of blessings, but because of His grace and mercy.

The Lord God is "merciful and gracious, longsuffering, and abounding in goodness and truth" (Exod. 34:6). Moreover, God's grace is associated with love, mercy, truth, compassion and patience. Although the grace of God is always free and undeserved, we cannot take it for granted. As a matter of fact, God's grace can only be received through repentance and faith; and must be humbly sought through the prayer of faith (Mal. 1:9). The only way to salvation for any person is " through the grace of the Lord Jesus Christ" (Acts 15:11). Moreover, recipients of God's grace must have faith and trust in the mercy and favor of God, even when it is undeserved (Rom. 4:16; Gal. 2:16). In like manner, God blesses those who belong to him by giving them life, riches, fruitfulness and abundance (Gen. 1:22, 28). His greatest blessing to us is in turning us from our iniquities (Acts 3:26); and forgiving our sins (Rom. 4:7, 8).

In Ephesians chapter one we read: "Blessed be the God and Father of our Lord Jesus Christ, who has blessed us with all spiritual blessings in heavenly places in Christ. According as he has chosen us in him before the foundation of the world ... Having predestined us unto the adoption of children by Jesus Christ to himself according to the good pleasure of his will. Having made known unto us the mystery of his will, according to his good pleasure which he has purposed in himself. That in the dispensation of the fullness of times, he might gather together in one all things in Christ, both which are in heaven, and which are on earth; even in him. In whom also we have obtained an inheritance, being predestinated according to the purpose of him who works all things after the counsel of his own will ... In whom ye also trusted ... in whom also after that ye believed, ye were sealed with that Holy Spirit of promise" (vv. 3-5, 9-11, 13).

In order to receive God's Grace, we must be in his sovereign will and purpose. For we know that all things work together for good to them who love God; for those who are called according to His purpose; for those who are predestined to be conformed to the image of His Son; and for those whom He has justified and will someday glorify. He spared not his own Son, but delivered Him up for us all, and will freely give us all things. Therefore, in all things we are more than conquerors through Him that loved us.

And, nothing shall separate us from the love of God, which is in Christ Jesus our Lord (Rom. 8:28-39). Paul proclaims the Word of God and preached to the Gentiles the unsearchable riches of Christ; And made known the mystery of Eternal life, which was from the beginning of the world hid in God, who created all things by Jesus Christ: "According to the eternal purpose which he purposed in Christ Jesus our Lord" (Eph. 3:8, 9, 11). Eyes have not seen and ears have not heard what God has prepared for those who wait for Him (Isa. 64:4).

Some of the Spiritual Blessings that Christians enjoy include the following: (1) We are a chosen generation, a royal priesthood, an holy nation, and a peculiar people; who have been called out of darkness into the marvellous light; and now have obtained mercy (I Pet. 2:9, 10). We belong to Christ, for we are bought with a price and have the Holy Ghost living inside of us (I Cor.6:19, 20). We are called with a holy calling, according to His own purpose and grace which was given to us in Christ Jesus, before the world began (II Tim. 1:9). (2) We have forgiveness of sins, according to the riches of His grace and we have obtained an eternal inheritance through Jesus Christ (Eph.1:7, 11). (3) The blood of Jesus cleanses us from all sin. Hence, if we confess our sins, He is faithful and just to forgive our sins, and to cleanse us from all unrighteousness (I John 1:7, 9). (4) We have the peace of God, which passes all understanding and which keeps our hearts and minds through Jesus Christ (Phil. 4:7).

The third Promise is Eternal Life and Salvation through Jesus Christ: "For God so loved the world that he gave his only begotten Son that whosoever believes on him should not perish, but have everlasting life. For God sent not his Son into the world to condemn the world; but that the world through him might be saved" (John 3:16, 17). "To them who by patient continuance in well doing seek for glory and honor and immortality, eternal life" (Rom. 2:7). "For ye are dead, and your life is hid with Christ in God. When Christ, who is our life, shall appear, then shall ye also appear with him in glory" (Col. 3:4). Salvation is a work of God by which He saves man from the eternal doom of sin. In salvation, God gives to us the riches of His Grace through the gift of salvation and eternal life. Salvation is not only forgiveness of sin, it is also eternal life. Salvation means to be "born again," and it is a free gift from God and not a work of man.

God invites all people everywhere to repent of their sins, to believe in Jesus Christ, and to accept the offer of forgiveness and salvation found in the Gospel. Jesus came not to call the righteous, but sinners to repentance (Lk. 5:32). God the Father planned the scheme of redemption for man and God the Son executed it through His death, burial, resurrection, and ascension. Hence, Paul pleads with the Corinthians to be reconciled to God: "But all things are of God, who reconciled us to himself through Christ ... Now then we are ambassadors for Christ, as though God did beseech you by us: we pray you in Christ's stead, be ye reconciled to God" (II Cor.5:18, 20). According to Hebrews 2:9, by the grace of God, Christ tasted death for every man. Likewise, in I Timothy 2:4, we learn that God will have all men to be saved, and to come to the knowledge of the truth. God invites man-kind everywhere to "look unto me and be saved, all the ends of the earth" (Isa. 45:22). "And come unto me, all that labor and are heavy laden, and I will give you rest. Take my yolk upon you and learn of me and you will find rest unto your souls" (Mat.11:28, 29).

God's plan of redemption is the only way to receive salvation and eternal life. We have redemption through the shed blood of Christ, the forgiveness of sins, according to the riches of God's grace (Eph. 1:7). In Titus 2:11, we read: "for the grace of God that brings salvation has appeared to all men." Since God desires the salvation of all men, He does everything in His Power to bring everyone of us to a saving knowledge of Himself, but He does not force our will. He gives us so many chances to receive the free gift of salvation and eternal life. We cannot earn it and we do not deserve it, but thanks be to God for our salvation. For whosoever shall call upon the name of the Lord shall be saved (Rom. 10:13). The Lord Jesus assures all who hunger and thirst for righteousness that they shall be filled (Mat. 5:6). Moreover, God promises eternal life to all who have accepted the Lord Jesus; those who have been born again, and regenerated by the power of the Holy Spirit. Jesus says: "Be thou faithful unto death, and I will give thee a crown of life" (Rev. 2:10). "To him that overcometh will I grant to sit with me in my throne, even as I also overcame, and am set down with my Father in his throne" (Rev. 3:21). Jesus is the way, the truth and the life, no man comes to the Father except by Him (John 14:6).

People everywhere must understand that Jesus is the only way that we can receive eternal life and spend eternity with Him in heaven. Everyone is saved in the identically same way, that is through Christ Jesus, there is no other way! There is no back door or side door salvation, you must come in at the door, which is Christ. Jesus says: "Verily, verily, I say unto you, he that entered not by the door into the sheepfold, but climbeth up some other way, the same is a thief and a robber. Then said Jesus unto them again, Verily, verily I say unto you, I am the door of the sheep. I am the door: by me if any man enter in, he shall be saved" (John 10:1, 7, 9). Hence, to any reader of this book who has not accepted the Lord Jesus Christ as your Saviour, I strongly encourage you to do it today, tomorrow may be too late.

The free will of man suggests that man is free to accept or reject the Grace and blessings of God and the free offer of salvation. As we know, God made every human being a free moral agent. This means that every individual must make his or her own decision. But Jesus desires that all will choose salvation and eternal life: "For this is good and acceptable in the sight of God our Saviour; who will have all men to be saved, and to come unto the knowledge of truth" (I Tim. 2:3, 4). "The Lord is not slack concerning his promise, as some men count slackness; but is longsuffering to usward, not willing that any should perish, but that all should come to repentance" (II Pet. 3:9). Jesus has made many admonitions to man to seek salvation. A few invitations familiar to most of us are cited below: "Ask, and it shall be given you; seek and ye shall find; knock and it shall be opened unto you" (Lk. 11:9). "Behold, I stand at the door, and knock: if any man hear my voice, and open the door, I will come in to him, and will sup with him, and he with me" (Rev.3:20). "And the Spirit and the bride say, Come. And he that heareth, let him say, Come. And let him that is athirst, come. And whosoever will, let him take the water of life freely" (Rev. 22:17).

No believer should be afraid or doubtful of his Eternal Salvation in Jesus Christ, considering we have God's Promise of it and He cannot lie. "Therefore the redeemed of the Lord shall return, and come with singing unto Zion; and everlasting joy shall be upon their head:

they shall obtain gladness and joy; and sorrow and mourning shall flee away. I, even I, am he that comforts you: ... the Lord thy maker, that has stretched forth the heavens, and laid the foundations of the earth .."(Isa. 51:11-13). This promise, along with the unwavering faith of the believer is sufficient to stay the soul against discouragements, temptations and sorrows. Hence, God the Son has dignified man and abased Himself, by taking man's nature upon Him (Heb. 2:16). We should not feel cast down or disquieted in our spirit, because Christ who is our Elder Brother has taken on human nature for no other purpose, than for our salvation. "For to this end Christ both died, and rose, and revived, that he might be Lord both of the dead and the living" (Rom. 14:9).

The Promises of God are sure and by divine Wisdom and Love are suitable and appropriate to the particular needs, and are relevant in all the cases of the Saints, whether "Spiritual or Temporal" in nature. Moreover, the Lord Jesus Christ, who is the Great Shepherd and Physician of souls, in whom the Godhead dwells bodily, and who has all power both in heaven and in earth has promised to uphold His people in all their trials and afflictions. In all their troubles, Christians must learn to wait on God for the fulfillment of His Promises, for He is faithful and will not fail you or forsake you.

Temporal Promises pertain to those life situations and conditions that believers face, and which require assistance, support, protection, aide and comfort. Our Christianity does not shield us from sufferings, trials, and tribulations. To suffer means to endure agony, affliction, distress, and intense pain or sorrow. Jesus Himself had to suffer for our salvation. "For it became him, for whom are all things, and by whom are all things, in bringing many sons unto glory, to make the captain of their salvation perfect through suffering" (Heb. 2:10). "For even hereunto were ye called: because Christ also suffered for us, leaving us an example that ye should follow his steps" (I Pet. 2:21). In that Jesus Himself has suffered being tempted, He is able to relieve those who are tempted (Heb. 2:18). When God saves us, He begins a work which has the ultimate goal of conforming us to the image of His Son. The Word of God tells us that some suffering is for the purpose of shaping and refining the children of God (I Pet.1:6; 5:10). In addition, suffering has the potential of demonstrating the power of

God (II Cor. 12:9). Therefore, those who suffer are in a unique position of blessings, comfort, and consolation (II Cor. 1:3 - 5). It is in times of crises, tragedies, and stressful situations that we as Christians must draw on our faith and the Promises of God in the Scriptures. God never promised us that we would not face trials and tribulations, but God promised to be with us through them all. The grace, love and mercy of God is not only able to redeem us, but it is able to keep us, as well. We must learn to be content, whatever our state or condition. Trials and tribulations have the effect in our lives, not only of teaching us, but also of allowing us to experience the goodness of the Lord every day; for assuredly we know that all things work together for the good of them that fear and love the Lord. Paul states that the peace of God which passes all understanding shall keep your hearts and minds through Jesus Christ (Phil 4:7). Likewise, Jesus promises: "Peace I leave with you, my peace I give unto you: not as the world gives, give I unto you. Let not your heart be troubled, neither let it be afraid" (John 14:27). For we know that the wisdom of the spirit is life and peace (Rom. 8:6); and peace is the inheritance of Christians.

There are specific promises that God the Father and God the Son have made to Christians in specific situation and conditions. Within the context of our discussion, we will focus on the following three: (1) In mourning; (2) In trials and afflictions; and (3) When alone and forsaken. "For our light affliction, which is but for a moment, worketh for us a far more exceeding and eternal weight of glory ... For the things which are seen are temporal; but the things which are not seen are eternal" (II Cor. 4:17, 18).

One of the Promises of the Father in regards to mourning was prophesied by Isaiah who proclaims God's promise: "To comfort all that mourn; To appoint unto them that mourn in Zion, to give unto them beauty for ashes, the oil of joy for mourning, the garment of praise for the spirit of heaviness; that they might be called trees of righteousness. For your shame ye shall have double; and for confusion they shall rejoice in their portion; therefore in their land they shall possess the double: everlasting joy shall be unto them" (Isa. 61:2, 3, 7). Further, the prophet Isaiah proclaims: "I have seen his ways, and will heal him: I will lead him also and restore comforts unto him and to his mourners. I create the fruit of the lips; Peace, peace to him that is far off, and to him that is near, saith the Lord; and I will heal him" (Isa. 57:18, 19). The prophet Jeremiah exclaims that God will turn their mourning into joy, will comfort them, and make them rejoice from their sorrow (Jer. 31:13). And Jesus taught the multitudes that: "Blessed are they that mourn: for they shall be comforted" (Matt. 5:4). Humble yourselves in the sight of God and He will lift you up (Ja. 4:9, 10).

Jesus tasted of humanity and was touched with the feelings of our infirmities. He was in all points tested as we are, and yet without sin (Heb. 4:15). Hence, the Prophet Isaiah sums up His work on our behalf as follows: "He is despised and rejected of men; a man of sorrows, and acquainted with grief ... Surely he has borne our griefs, and carried our sorrows; smitten of God and afflicted. But he was wounded for our transgressions, he was bruised for our iniquities: the chastisement of our peace was upon him; and with his stripes we are healed. All we like sheep have gone astray; we have turned every one to his own way; and the Lord has laid on him the iniquity of us all" (Isa. 53:3-6).

When a loved one dies, Christians should not mourn as the unsaved who have no hope. We should console ourselves with the knowledge that believers shall be eternally happy: "And they shall be mine, saith the Lord of hosts, in that day when I make up my jewels; and I will spare them, as a man spares his own son that serves him" (Mal. 3:17). But God, who is rich in love and mercy has raised us up together; and made us sit together in heavenly places in Christ Jesus, showing His Grace toward us. For by Grace we are saved through faith; and not of ourselves, it is the gift of God. (Eph. 2:4-8).

In times of sorrow, we can comfort ourselves in knowing: "that the everlasting God, the Lord, the Creator of the ends of the earth, faints not, neither is weary ... there is no searching of his understanding. He gives power to the faint; and to them that have no might he increases strength ... But they that wait upon the Lord shall renew their strength; they shall mount up with wings as eagles; they shall run, and not be weary; and they shall walk, and not faint" (Isa. 40:28, 29, 31). We are admonished to be afflicted, and mourn, and weep: let your laughter be turned to mourning, and your joy to heaviness. Weeping may endure for a night, but joy comes in the morning (Ps. 30:5). As pertains to mourning, the prophet Jeremiah writes: "Thus saith the Lord, refrain thy voice from weeping, and thine eyes from tears; for thy work shall be rewarded, and there is hope in thine end" (Jer. 31:15-17). In all of our sorrows we should remember the words of our Lord who promises that when you weep and lament, He will turn your sorrow into joy, give you rejoicing of your heart and joy that no man can take away from you (John 16:20, 22).

As pertains to general afflictions, God promises to save, redeem, bare, and carry us all the days of old (Isa. 63:9). "There shall no evil befall you, neither shall any plague come nigh your dwelling. For he shall give his angels charge over you, to keep you in all your ways. They shall bear you up in their hands, lest you dash your foot against a stone. You shall tread upon the lion and adder: the young lion and the dragon shall you trample under feet" (Ps. 91:10-13). In each and every one of our afflictions, the Lord gives the believer the strength to overcome the affliction. Hence, David declares: "But I will sing of thy power; yea, I will sing aloud of thy mercy in the morning: for thou hast been my defence and refuge in the day of my trouble" (Ps.59:16).

Some of God's Promises relative to specific trials and afflictions are as follows: "When thou passes through the waters, I will be with thee; and through the rivers, they shall not overflow thee: when thou walkest through the fire, thou shall not be burned; neither shall the flame kindle thee. Fear not: for I am with thee" (Isa. 43:2, 5). "He shall call upon me, and I will answer him: I will be with him in trouble; I will deliver him and honor him. With long life will I satisfy him and shew him my salvation" (Ps. 91:15, 16). "For the Lord God is a sun and shield: the Lord will give grace and glory: no good thing will he withhold from them that walk uprightly" (Ps. 84:11).

Relative to God's Promise to those who are alone and forsaken, He promises that: "When my father and my mother forsake me, then the Lord will take me up" (Ps. 27:10). Further, the prophet Isaiah proclaims: "Can a woman forget her sucking child, that she should not have compassion on the son of her womb? yea, they may forget, yet will I not forget thee. Behold, I have graven thee upon the palms of my hands; thy walls are continually before me" (Isa. 49:15, 16). God promises that when you are forgotten, forsaken and outcast, He will restore your health and heal all your wounds (Jer. 30:14, 17). Friends may move away or onto other friends. Sometimes we find ourselves alone when our friends or loved ones die. The Scriptures admonish us to "be content with such things that we have: for he hath said, *I will never leave thee, nor forsake thee*" (Heb. 13:5). As the songwriter says: "What a friend we have in Jesus, all our sins and griefs to bear, what a privilege to carry, everything to God in prayer." And I recall the words of another song that gives encouragement to the lonely: "There's not a friend like the lowly Jesus, no not one, no not one." In reality, Jesus is our best friend and He will never leave us or forsake us. We are to be strong and of good courage, we are not to be fearful or afraid; for the Lord God, will not fail us or forsake us (Deut. 31:6). There is great encouragement in the Proverbs of Solomon, who says that a man that has friends must first show himself to be friendly, and Jesus is a friend that sticks closer than a brother (Prov. 18:24). Moreover, a friend loves at all times (Prov. 17:17).

Whatever the trial or affliction, God either suffered it to happen or He allowed it to happen. Sometimes believers are afflicted and chastised to test their faith and patience in God's promises to them in their afflictions. Whatever the trial or test, the believer has the assurance that God is with you and He has already provided a method of escape. When believers cry unto God in their trouble, He saves them from their distresses and delivers them from their destructions (Ps.107:19, 20). "Behold the eye of the Lord is upon them that fear him, upon them that hope in his mercy; To deliver their soul from death, and to keep them alive in famine. Our soul waits for the Lord: he is our help and our shield" (Ps. 33:18-20). Job exclaims the following: "For he makes sore, and binds up: he wounds, and his hands make whole" (5:18). The Lord upholds all that fall and raises up all that are bowed down. He is near all that call upon Him in truth; He will fulfill the desires of them that fear Him; and He will hear their cry and save them (Ps. 145:14-19).

In order to enjoy the promises and blessings of God, there are specific duties that God requires of us. The duties to God on man's part are expressed in various ways in Scripture. Moses under the Law advises the people of Israel of their duty toward God in this manner: "And now, Israel, what does the Lord thy God require of thee, but to fear the Lord thy God, to walk in all his ways, and to love him, and to serve the Lord thy God with all thy heart and with all thy soul, To keep the commandments of the Lord, and his statues, which I command thee this day for thy good?" (Deut.10:12, 13). In like manner, the Prophet Micah declares the following: "He has shewed thee, O man, what is good; and what does the Lord require of thee, but to do justly, and to love mercy, and to walk humbly with thy God?" (Mic. 6:8). The duty of Christians under the Gospel are spelled out in numerous New Testament Scriptures. Two examples are stated below: "Having therefore these promises, dearly beloved, let us cleanse ourselves from all filthiness of the flesh, and spirit, perfecting holiness in the fear of God" (II Cor. 7:1). "Let your light so shine before men, that they may see your good works, and glorify your Father which in heaven" (Matt. 5:16). Christians are to present their bodies a living sacrifice, holy, and acceptable to God, which is your reasonable service. And be not conformed to this world: but be transformed by the renewing of your mind, that you may prove what is that good and acceptable, and perfect will of God (Rom. 12:1, 2).

CHAPTER 9

THE MYSTERY OF ETERNAL LIFE

Synopsis

Chapter nine elucidates and examines scriptures which define what eternal life is, explains who shall receive it, and which declare that the saved will be transformed to the image of Jesus Christ.

Eternal Life refers to the future inheritance in Jesus Christ that is granted by God as a gift to all believer's who die in Christ. The term "Everlasting Life" denotes the blessed character of the life that will be enjoyed endlessly in the future. Jesus made it clear that eternal life comes only to those who have made a total commitment to Him. This Holy estate and inheritance of the Godly is incorruptible and not subject to changes or alterations. The Apostle Peter describes the blessed state as follows: Blessed be the God and Father of our Lord Jesus Christ, who according to His abundant Mercy, has begotten us again unto a lively hope, by the resurrection of Jesus Christ from the dead; unto an inheritance, incorruptible and undefiled, and that faded not away, reserved in the Heavens for us, who are kept by the power of God, through faith unto salvation (I Pet.1:3-5). Eternal Life is that blessed state, a treasure laid up for the Saints of God, where moth cannot consume and thieves cannot break through and steal. Herein is a state of complete happiness, wherein there is fullness of joy, and pleasures forevermore.

Eternal life means more than eternal existence, rather, it is eternal fellowship with God through faith in Jesus Christ. Jesus taught: (1) "Search the scriptures; for in them ye think ye have eternal life" (John 5:39a). (2) "And this is the will of him that sent me, that every one which sees the Son, and believes on him, may have everlasting life ..." (John 6:40). (3) "He that believes on me has everlasting life" (John 6:47). (4) "I am the resurrection, and the life: he that believes in me, though he were dead, yet shall he live: And whosoever lives and believes in me shall never die" (John 11:25, 26). John uses similar symbolism to depict the meaning of life: "In him was life; and the life was the light of men" (John 1:4). The Prophet Isaiah references everlasting life in the following manner: "The sun shall be no more thy light by day; neither for brightness shall the moon give light unto thee: but the Lord shall be unto thee an everlasting light, and thy God thy glory. Thy sun shall no more go down; neither shall thy moon withdraw itself: for the Lord shall be thine everlasting light, and the days of thy mourning shall be ended" (Isa.60:19, 20). And the Apostle John writing in the book of Revelation declares: "These are they which came out of great tribulation, and have washed their robes, and made them white in the blood of the Lamb. Therefore are they before the throne of God, and serve him day and night in his temple: and he that sits on the throne shall dwell among them. They shall hunger no more, neither thirst any more; neither shall the sun light on them, nor any heat. For the Lamb which is in the midst of the throne shall feed them, and shall lead them unto living fountains of waters: And God shall wipe away all tears from their eyes; and there shall be no more death, neither sorrow, nor crying, neither shall there be any more pain: for the former things are passed away" (Rev. 7:14-17; 21:4).

Therefore, salvation, eternal happiness, the incorruptible and undefiled inheritance of all things, and the inseparable fellowship of the Holy Trinity, angels and saints is the undeniable prize that we will receive at the end of life's race. Wherefore, seeing that we also are compassed about with so great a cloud of witnesses, let us lay aside every weight, and the sin which so easily besets us, and let us run with patience the race that is set before us. Looking unto Jesus the author and finisher of our faith; who for the joy that was set before him endured the cross, despising the shame, and is set down at the right hand of the throne of God. Consider Him that endured such contradiction of sinners against himself, lest you be weary in your minds (Heb. 12:1-3). Thus, our salvation is freely of God's pure love in Christ Jesus. For Christ made and redeemed the world without man's help. Not by works of righteousness that we have done, but according to His mercy he saves us, by the washing of the regeneration, and renewing of the Holy Ghost. Which He shed on us abundantly through Jesus Christ our Savior; that being justified by His grace, we are made heirs of the hope of eternal life (Titus 3:5-7). Hence, the future estate of the redeemed is far more excellent than his first creation.

The mystery of eternal life which was hid from the beginning of the world is this, that the Son of God who knew no sin, gave Himself unto death, to pay the price for our sins (Eph. 3:9). The mystery which has been hid for ages and for generations is now made manifest to the saints. To whom God has made known what is the riches of the glory of this mystery among the Gentiles; which is Christ in you the hope of Glory (Col.1:26, 27). Eyes have not seen, ears have not heard, nor has it entered into the hearts of men, the things that God has prepared of those who love Him (I Cor. 2:9). Basically, the mystery of eternal life reveals the unsearchable dimensions of the love of God to sinners, in his eternal purpose of redeeming the world by Jesus Christ, and opening the way for eternal fellowship with Him. Jesus came into the world to teach the gospel, and the mystery of this great salvation. The mystery of love and redemption of man, is magnified by the obedience and suffering of Christ. The greatest of sins cannot hinder God's love for us. The Word of God tell us that though your sins may be as scarlet, they shall be as white as snow, though they be red as crimson, they shall be as wool (Isa. 1:18).

Behold what manner of love the Father has bestowed upon us that we should be called the sons of God. And now we are the sons of God, and it does not yet appear what we shall be, but we know that, when He shall appear, we shall be like him; for we shall see him as He is (I John 3:1, 2). In this was manifested the love of God toward us, because God sent His only begotten Son into the world, that we through Him might live. Herein is love revealed, not that we loved God, but that He loved us, and sent His Son to be the propitiation for our sins (I John 4:9, 10). And this is the record, that God has given to us eternal life, and this life is in His Son. He that has the Son has life; and he that does not have the Son of God does not have life. The Scriptures are written so that all who believe on the name of the Son of God may know that you have eternal life, and so that you may believe on the name of the Son of God (I John 5:9 -13).

CHAPTER 10

THE ESSENTIAL REQUIREMENTS OF ETERNAL LIFE

Synopsis

The first section of chapter ten reiterates God's promise to send a redeemer and examines God's plan of redemption for mankind. It explains Christ's sufferings for the sins of mankind and the necessity for regeneration, which means to be born of the Spirit of God. The bulk of this chapter is focused on an in-depth examination of three essential requirements for eternal life which are: (1) Salvation; (2) Repentance; and (3) Faith. Each of these requirements is defined and explained in clear terms, with relevant scriptures to substantiate the Christian belief. Throughout the chapter, the invitation to salvation is given.

In order to redeem man from the penalty of sin, the Lord Jesus Christ entered the world exactly as the Scriptures had said; he lived; died on the cross; and ascended back into glory. God the Son, who is the second manifestation of the Holy Trinity, knew the consequences of man's sin and willingly came down in the form of humanity to pay the price for man's redemption. As a man, He lived the most perfect life ever known. And He died to take away the sins of the world and to become the Savior of man. Then He rose from the dead and the good news is that He is alive today and forevermore. Christ arose from the grave to conquer sin and death, and to assure us of the resurrected life. When on the cross, Jesus cried out "it is finished." By this statement, He meant that the battle had been fought and the victory had been won over Satan and the power of death.

Moreover, by His suffering, death and resurrection, Christ became not only justice for man, but He has also redeemed man from the future wrath of God, secured for man eternal happiness in the presence of God, and He has established a pattern of patience and obedience for all believers to follow. Hence, in prophesying in The Old Testament of Christ's suffering for the sins of man-kind, the prophet Isaiah proclaims that He shall grow up before him as a tender plant, and as a root out of dry ground: he has no form or comeliness; and when we shall see him, there is no beauty that we should desire him. He is despised and rejected of men: a man of sorrows and acquainted with grief: and we hid as it were our faces from him; he was despised and we esteemed him not. Surely He has borne our griefs, and carried our sorrows; smitten of God, and afflicted. But he was wounded for our transgressions, he was bruised for our iniquities: the chastisement of our peace was upon him; and with his stripes we are healed. He was oppressed and he was afflicted, yet he opened not his mouth; he is brought as a lamb to the slaughter, and as a sheep before her shearers is dumb, so he opened not his mouth. For he was cut off out of the land of the living: and for the transgression of my people was he stricken. And he made his grave with the wicked, and with the rich in his death; because he had done no violence, neither was any deceit in his mouth. Yet it pleased the Lord to bruise him and put him to grief and make his soul an offering for sin. He shall see the travail of his soul, and shall be satisfied: for his righteous servant shall justify many; for he shall bear their iniquities (Isa. 53:2-11).

Because Christ suffered leaving us an example that we should follow His steps: who did not sin, neither was guile found in His mouth, who when He was reviled, reviled not again; when He suffered, He threatened not; but committed Himself to Him who judges righteously. Who Himself bare our sins in His own body on the tree, that we being dead to sins, should live unto righteousness: by whose stripes we were healed. And are now returned to the Shepherd and Bishop of our souls (I Pet. 2:21-25). When we think about all that God has done for us, we should run swiftly to him with thankful hearts and spirits. Furthermore, if there is any reader of this book who does not know the Lord Jesus in the pardon of their sins, they should come to Jesus right now and cry out "what must I do to be saved?" In answering this question, Jesus made known to Nicodemus the necessity of regeneration; which means to be born by the Spirit. Jesus answered and said unto him, "Verily, verily, I say unto thee, Except a man be born again, he cannot see the Kingdom of God" (John 3:3). There may be someone who needs to know how to receive eternal life. Hence, the next part of our discussion will focus on what I believe are the three essential requirements of eternal life and which are stated as follows: (1) Salvation; (2) Repentance; and (3) Faith.

Salvation

In general terms, salvation refers to deliverance from the power of sin or redemption from sin. In more specific terms, salvation is a doctrinal term which relates to the work of God by which He saves man-kind from the eternal doom of sin. The doctrine of salvation reached its fulfillment in the death of Christ on our behalf. The mission of the Son of God was to save the world from sin and the wrath of God (Matt.1:21; John 12:47; Rom. 5:9). God releases into our lives the power of Christ's resurrection (Rom 6:4), seals us (II Cor. 1:22) and gives us a foretaste of our future life as His children (Eph. 1:14). The death and resurrection of Christ offers everlasting life to all who will believe. I don't know why Jesus loves us so; but one thing I do know is that God commended his love for us, in that while we were yet sinners, Christ died for us (Rom 5:8). For God so loved the world, that He gave His only begotten Son, that whosoever believes in him should not perish, but shall have everlasting life (John 3:16). And now being justified by his blood, we shall be saved from wrath through Him. For if, when we were enemies, we were reconciled to God by the death of His Son, much more, being reconciled, we shall be saved by his life (Rom. 5:9-10). Hence, when the Spirit of God dwells inside of us, the same Spirit that raised Jesus from the dead will also quicken our mortal bodies and make us alive eternally.

Salvation is a work and an accomplishment of God. Jesus came into the world as promised in the Old Testament Scriptures to save sinners by His death on the cross, according to the deliberate will and plan of God. The ultimate purpose being to provide a way for sinners to obtain a right relationship with God and to receive the gift of eternal life. God's plan of salvation for man encompasses three stages: (1) Must believe and acknowledge the Lord Jesus Christ; (2) Must repent of sins; and (3) Must accept Christ's offer of forgiveness and salvation. Moreover, salvation is receive by grace through faith. This means that salvation is given by the grace of God on the basis of our belief in His Son. The fact that salvation is a gift of God to all who believe is made clear in Ephesians 2:8:"For by grace are ye saved through faith; and that not of yourselves: it is the gift of God." The second stage is to repent of sin; meaning to admit that you are a sinner and ask for God's forgiveness. An admission and a confession that you are a sinner is required, "for all have sinned and come short of the glory of God" (Rom. 3:23). But now being made free from sin, and now having become servants of God; you have your fruit unto holiness, and the end is everlasting life. For the wages of sin is death; but the gift of God is eternal life through Jesus our Lord (Rom. 6:23). The forgiveness of sin for the sinner is accomplished when the individual believes upon Christ and is a part of one's salvation. For the Christian, sin is forgiven not on the ground of believing unto salvation, but on the ground of confessing the sin. When you come to God and repent, He will save you. He always keeps his promises and He is not willing that any should perish.

God invites all people to repent; this connotation means that one must believe on the Lord Jesus Christ and accept the free offer of forgiveness of sin. Essentially, this involves confessing with your mouth and believing in your heart that Jesus is the Son of God and believing that God has raised Jesus from the dead. The Word of God teaches us that if you will confess with your mouth the Lord Jesus, and believe in your heart that God has raised him from the dead, you shall be saved. For with the heart man believes unto righteousness; and with the mouth confession is made unto salvation. For whosoever believes in the Lord Jesus shall not be ashamed and whosoever shall call upon the name of the Lord shall be saved (Rom.10:9-11, 13).

God's plan of salvation brings deliverance, meaning that God will bring us through as long as we walk day by day with Him. The Christian walk requires us to commit each day to Christ and invite the Holy Spirit to take control of our lives and help us to live each day in accordance with God's Word. Christians must confess their sins and be forgiven. For if we confess our sins, He is faithful and just to forgive our sins and to cleanse us from all unrighteousness (I John 1:9). Therefore, the saved have a new birth, are regenerated, have a new life, and are built on Christ the foundation and nourisher of life. Jesus says: "I am the vine, ye are the branches: He that abideth in me, and I in him, the same bringeth forth much fruit: for without me ye can do nothing" (John 15:5).

Repentance

Repentance is defined as a turning away from sin, disobedience, or rebellion and a turning back to God. Jesus says: "I am not come to call the righteous, but sinners to repentance" (Matt. 9:13; Lk. 5:32). In a more general sense, repentance means a change of mind and a feeling of remorse or regret for past conduct. Repentance is turning from wickedness and dead works (Acts 8:22) toward God and His glory (Acts 20:21; Rev. 16:9), eternal life (Acts 11:18); and a knowledge of the truth (II Tim. 2:25). True repentance is a "godly sorrow" for sin; an act of turning around and going in the opposite direction. Hence, true repentance involves a frank acknowledgment of the sin; sorrow for the sin; and a determination to forsake the sin. This type of repentance leads to a fundamental change in a person's relationship with God. Repentance is essential to eternal life because it is God's will and pleasure (Lk. 15:7-10; II Pet. 3:9), as well as His command (Mk. 6:12; Acts 17:30). Repentance is a free gift of God's sovereign love (Acts 5:31; 11:18; Rom. 2:4), without which we cannot be saved (Lk. 13:3).

Therefore, repentance is not only an essential requirement, it is also indispensable to salvation. John the Baptist preached repentance in the admonishment to "Repent ye for the Kingdom of heaven is at hand" (Matt.3:2). Furthermore, he declared to the multitudes to bear fruits worthy of repentance (Matt.3:8; Lk. 3:8). Very importantly,

Jesus began His public ministry by preaching repentance. From that time Jesus began to preach and to say: "Repent: for the kingdom of heaven is at hand" (Matt. 4:17). Also, He expanded the message to include the good news of salvation: "The time is fulfilled, and the kingdom of God is at hand. Repent and believe in the gospel" (Mk. 1:15). Jesus called sinners to repentance (Matt 9:13), and used Jonah as an example to teach repentance. "The men of Ninevah shall rise in judgment with this generation and shall condemn it: because they repented at the preaching of Jonas; and, behold, a greater Jonas is here" (Matt.12:41). The teachings of Christ reveal the fundamental truth that repentance and faith are both essential to salvation. Through repentance one turns from sin and by faith one turns to God in accepting the Lord Jesus Christ. Such a twofold turning or conversion is necessary for entry into the kingdom (Matt.18:3). Jesus cautions us that: "Unless you repent, you will all likewise perish (Lk. 13:3, 5). And He encourages us through these merciful words: "Likewise I say unto you, there is joy in the presence of the angels of God over one sinner that repents" (Lk. 15:10).

Moreover, after Jesus' death and resurrection, repentance and faith were preached by the apostles. Peter in preaching repentance said unto them: "Repent, and be baptized every one of you in the name of Jesus Christ for the remission of sins, and ye shall receive the gift of the Holy Ghost. Repent ye therefore, and be converted, that your sins may be blotted out" (Acts 2:38; 3:19). Similarly, Peter, John and Philip preached repentance in Samaria saying: "Repent therefore of this thy wickedness, and pray God, if perhaps the thought of thine heart may be forgiven thee" (Acts 8:22). Thus Paul preached repentance to the Ephesians testifying both to the Jews and also to the Greeks, repentance toward God, and faith toward our Lord Jesus Christ (Acts 20:21). Additionally, Paul spoke concerning "godly sorrow" in his statement that godly sorrow works repentance to salvation never to be regretted; but the sorrow of the world works to death (II Cor 7:10).

Godly sorrow is different from mere sorrow or remorse. Hence, just feeling bad is not repentance, nor is it godly sorrow. More appropriately godly sorrow produces true repentance and represents one's feelings about what sin is in relation to God. One must recognize that it is impossible to please God as long as there is sin in any area of one's life.

It takes both repentance and faith to be saved. Repentance involves introspection or taking an honest look at oneself and then turning from or forsaking one's sinful ways. Whereas, faith involves a looking above and turning to God through Jesus Christ. The three means by which repentance or turning is evidenced in behavior are as follows: (1) an intellectual repentance-or a change of mind; (2) an emotional repentance-or a change of heart; and (3) a volitional repentance-or a change in the will.

The necessity of repentance may be summarized as follows: (1) God commands it (Acts 17:30); (2) Unless men repent, they will perish (Lk.13:3, 5); (3) Repentance is the first response demanded of men, if they are to respond to the Gospel of Jesus Christ (Acts 2:38); (4) Repentance is a condition for cleansing (Isa. 6:5); (5) Repentance is a requirement for forgiveness (Lk. 24:47); (6) Repentance is a requirement for salvation (Acts 26:18); (7) Repentance is a requirement for entry into the kingdom of heaven (Matt. 4:17); (8) Repentance is a requirement for eternal life (Acts 11:18); (9) Repentance is a condition for escaping the judgment of God upon sin (Acts 17:30, 31).

Faith

Faith is defined as a sincere belief in or a confident attitude toward God, involving a personal commitment to his will for one's life. Repentance, or the initial phase of conversion, is an act of the will which causes one to turn away from sin. Paul refers to this step as "repentance toward God" (Acts 20:21). Hence, faith is the second phase of conversion, which Paul refers to as "faith toward the Lord Jesus Christ" (Acts 20:21). It is faith in the Lord Jesus Christ that saves us: " For by grace are we saved through faith (Eph. 2:8). Faith in our Redeemer, Jesus Christ brings about a transformation in the life of the believer. Faith takes hold of the repentant heart and leads the person to the merciful and forgiving God. To place total trust in Jesus and his power to save means placing total faith in Christ for eternal salvation. Hence, faith is absolutely essential to salvation. Paul says: "I am not ashamed of the gospel of Christ: for it is the power of God

unto salvation to everyone that believes. For therein is the righteousness of God revealed from faith to faith: as it is written, *The just shall
live by faith*" (Rom. 1:16, 17).

Furthermore, faith is a thought in the mind or spirit of the believer,
which has its allegiance in our Lord and Savior, Jesus Christ. You
must first believe that He exists; and second that He can perform what
you are trusting and believing Him to do. Faith takes the power out of
your hand and places it in the hand of the person that you have the
allegiance to. Essentially, this means that you are at the mercy of the
person in whom you are trusting. Therefore faith becomes trust and
reliance on God. Trust indicates your belief in God; whereas, reliance
connotes you approval of what God is going to do, without your trying
to tell Him when or how to do it. In order to have faith, one must be
informed of the saving power of accepting Jesus as Lord. Therefore,
it is impossible to have faith apart from some verse or passage from
the Word of God. Hence, the Bible says that "Faith comes by hearing
and hearing by the Word of God" (Rom. 10:17). In actuality, a person
realizes faith and the power of faith by knowing the source of faith.
Moreover, faith involves receiving (believing in) Jesus Christ. And
receiving Christ means trusting Him for salvation.

Before we proceed further into our discussion about faith; we must
clarify that faith is not based on visible evidence, nor is it grounded in
your emotions. The Scriptures tell us, first of all that faith is the
substance of things hoped for, the evidence of things not seen (Heb.
11:1). Stated in a different way, we can say that faith is being sure of
what you are believing God to do, even when there is no evidence in
sight. Second, although faith involves emotions; faith is not rooted in
your emotions. As we previously discussed, emotions pertain to your
feelings and are a part of your flesh. You may feel emotions such as,
happy, sad, anger, love, hate, and so forth; but your faith must be
grounded in objective fact. Jesus Christ is the object of our faith and
He is the objective fact on which our faith must be based. Since faith
is a spiritual belief, a person with faith has the spiritual insight to rely
on God and his Word even though you cannot see what you are
praying or hoping for. A person with faith will receive by faith what
one cannot see. This lets us know that faith cannot be a response to
evidence; but it must be a response to God and to God alone. Hence,

your faith is between you and God and it is never based on what is done or performed in the material realm. To the contrary, your faith must be based on God's personal disclosure of Himself to you. In other words, you must have a personal encounter with God and you must get to know Him for yourself and then you can receive by faith what God has promised.

Saving faith is trust and reliance in a divine person, who is our Redeemer, Jesus Christ. Sincere saving faith involves a personal attachment to Christ and a commitment to Him. Saving faith involves personally depending on the completed work of Christ's sacrifice on the cross as the only basis for forgiveness of sin and entrance into heaven. Moreover, saving faith is a surrendering of one's life and following Christ in obedience to His commands. Hence Paul proclaims: "For which cause I also suffer these things: nevertheless I am not ashamed: for I know whom I have believed, and am persuaded that he is able to keep that which I have committed unto him against that day" (II Tim. 1:12).

Faith is a part of the Christian experience from beginning to end. Faith is taking God at his Word. In our prayer life, faith is the confidence that we have in Him, that if we ask anything according to his will, He hears us (I John 5:14). Faith pleases God, for without faith it is impossible to please Him, for he who comes to God must believe that He is, and that He is a rewarder of those who diligently seek Him (Heb. 11:6). Faith is accepted by God in the place of righteousness which no human being could have or achieve. Moreover, the blessing of Abraham came on the Gentiles through Jesus Christ; that we might receive the promise of the Spirit through faith (Gal. 3:14). Hence, God has chosen the poor of this world who are rich in faith, and heirs of the kingdom which He has promised to them that love him (Ja. 2:5). A life of faith is a life of total trust knowing that all things work together for good to them that love God (Rom, 8:28). For we walk by faith and not by sight (II Cor. 5:7).

Faith is an intimate personal relationship with our Lord and Savior, Jesus Christ. Through faith, we come into a relationship with God, through Jesus Christ, in which He commits Himself to us, not only in declaring us righteous, but also in making us truly good persons. Like repentance, faith is evidenced in three ways: First, in the understanding through which one is convinced of Christ's redemption of man-kind. Second, in the feelings by which the person rests calmly in God's saving love. And finally, in the will through which one shows devotion and reverence to our Lord and Savior, Jesus Christ. The "substance" and "evidence" of faith are in the Word of God. Therefore, we believe in Him whom we have not seen, yet we love, and even now we see Him not, yet we believe and we rejoice with joy unspeakable and full of glory: receiving the end of our faith, even the salvation of our souls (I Pet.1:8-9).

PART III

GOD THE HOLY SPIRIT GIVES COMFORT AND PEACE

CHAPTER 11

WHO IS GOD THE HOLY SPIRIT

Synopsis

The first section of this chapter examines and provides biblical proofs of who the Holy Spirit is. The Holy Spirit is conceptualized as follows: (1) as the mysterious power or presence of God in the earth, (2) as a 'Comforter' or 'Paraclete,' and (3) as an Advocator, Intercessor and Teacher. The middle part of the chapter lists some of the works of the Holy Spirit in the Old Testament and presents the Holy Spirit as Eternal, as a participant in the creation, as the breath of life and as the Spirit of God. The last section of the chapter discusses the role of the Holy Spirit in the birth, baptism, ministry, and resurrection of our Lord and Savior, Jesus Christ. At the baptism of Jesus Christ, the Holy Spirit descended upon Him like a dove.

The Holy Spirit is the third manifestation of the Holy Trinity. He is a person with all the attributes of God and He carries out the will of the Father and the Son. The Holy Spirit is the mysterious power or presence of God in nature, or within persons, and communities, inspiring or empowering them with qualities they otherwise would not possess. When Jesus Christ was on the earth, the Holy Spirit was not present, because there was no need for two manifestations of the

Godhead abiding in the earth at the same time. But Jesus promises His disciples that "I will not leave you comfortless, I will pray the Father, and He will send you another Comforter, who shall be with you, and shall dwell in you forever." Moreover, when Christ ascended back into heaven, God the Father sent the Holy Spirit in the name of Jesus Christ. Hence, Jesus says: "Nevertheless I tell you the truth; It is expedient for you that I go away; for if I go not away, the Comforter will not come unto you; but if I depart; I will send him unto you. When the Spirit of truth is come, he will guide you into all truth: for he shall not speak of himself; but whatsoever he shall hear, that shall he speak: and he will show you things to come" (John 16:7, 13).

Before Jesus left the earth, He gave the disciples soothing words of comfort. He promised them a Comforter who would console them in their sorrows, allay their doubts and fears, comfort them in their afflictions and stand as Christ's Vicar in the earth. "But the Comforter, which is the Holy Ghost, whom the Father will send in my name, he shall teach you all things, and bring all things to your remembrance, whatsoever I have said unto you. Peace I leave with you, my peace I give unto you: not as the world giveth, give I unto you. Let not your heart be troubled, neither let it be afraid" (John 14:26-27). The word "Comforter" or "Paraclete," means one who speaks in favor of, such as an advocate, intercessor, counselor and teacher. Therefore, the Holy Spirit gives to us; He intercedes with Jesus for us; He gives us what God has promised; He gives us grace, that is God's unmerited favor towards us; and He comforts us as no other power can do. Very importantly, He is an ever-present Comforter. Moreover, the Psalmist declares that "God is our refuge and strength, a very present help in trouble. Therefore, we will not fear though the earth be removed, and though the mountains be carried into the midst of the sea. The Lord of hosts is with us ; the God of Jacob is our refuge" (Ps. 46:1-2; 7). These words give us assurance that the Spirit of God is always present in us to comfort us in our distress and to help us in the time of trouble.

The Holy Spirit was present in the beginning and was a participant in the creation. Both the Hebrew word "ruach" and the Greek word "pneuma" express the movement of air, and may reasonably be translated as "wind," "storm," or "breeze." Nonetheless, the literal meaning is "breath," which by extension is translated to mean "principle of life," "center of vitality" or "dynamic activity." It is through the great miracle of creation that God transmits His breath to His creatures and, in the highest degree to man. Thus, the creation of the heavens above is ascribed to God's Spirit. The Scriptures state: "By his spirit he hath garnished the heavens; and his hand hath formed the crooked serpent" (Job 26:13). Likewise, the continuation of life processes are also ascribed to the Spirit of God. "Thou hidest thy face, they are troubled: thou takest away their breath, they die, and return to the dust. Thou sendest forth thy spirit, they are created: and thou renewest the face of the earth" (Ps. 104:29-30). Although the name "Holy Spirit" appears only three times in the Old Testament (Ps. 51:11; Isa. 63:10-11), the work of the Holy Spirit is apparent throughout. The Spirit is the energy of God in creation. And the Spirit of God moved upon the face of the waters (Gen. 1:2). God endowed man-kind with life by breathing into their nostrils the breath of life (Gen. 2:7). The breath of God is the Spirit of God. The Holy Spirit is the Spirit of God and God is the Holy Spirit. Moreover, in the Old Testament, the Holy Spirit was the special source of enablement for God's people. Hence, in the days of old, the Holy Spirit was responsible for most of the spectacular feats or acts that occurred (Joshua, Num. 27:18; Gideon, Jud. 6:34; Samson, Jud. 13:25; 14:6), to mention a few. These references indicate that the Holy Spirit did not indwell individuals; but rather that He came upon them (Num. 11:25), He poured out upon them (Prov. 1:23), He rested upon them (Num. 11:25, 26), and He left them as He willed (Jud. 14:6, 19). Moreover, the Holy Spirit was a special gift from God and He served a special purpose of God.

Within the sphere of Old Testament prophecy, the "Spirit" plays a prominent role. For example, David declares: "The Spirit of the Lord spoke by me, and His word was on my tongue" (II Sam. 23:2). Ezekiel claims that "the spirit entered into me when he spoke unto me" (Ezk. 2:2). Additionally, Ezekiel writes: "A new heart also will I give you, and a new spirit will I put within you. And I will put my spirit within you, and cause you to walk in my statues, and ye shall keep my judgments, and do them" (Ezk.36:26, 27). Moreover, the Psalmist prays: "Teach me to do thy will; for thou art my God: thy spirit is good; lead me into the land of uprightness" (Ps.143:10). Hence, there is the promise of God to pour out his Spirit upon all flesh: "and your sons and daughters shall prophesy, your old men shall dream dreams, your young men shall see visions" (Joel 2:28). Likewise, the Holy Spirit inspired Old Testament writers in the transmission of the Word of God. "For the prophecy came not in old time by the will of man; but holy men of God spake as they were moved by the Holy Ghost" (II Pet.1:21).

Therefore, the Old Testament writings prophesied of the coming of the Anointed One, the Righteous King, the Messiah. The Word of God tells us that the Holy Spirit was particularly instrumental in the creation of the incarnate Christ. "Now the birth of Jesus was on this wise: When Mary his mother was espoused to Joseph, before they came together, she was found with child of the Holy Ghost ... And the angel of the Lord appeared unto him in a dream, saying, Joseph, thou son of David, fear not to take unto thee Mary thy wife: for that which is conceived in her is of the Holy Ghost. And she shall bring forth a son, and thou shall call his name Jesus: for he shall save his people from their sins" (Mat.1:18, 20, 21). Hence, the prophecy of Isaiah in Chapter 11, verses 1 - 5 looks forward to the unity in working of the Holy Trinity: Father, Son and Holy Spirit in fulfilling the ministry of Jesus Christ. Moreover, the Holy Spirit inspired the prophet Isaiah to write: "And there shall come forth a rod out of the stem of Jesse, and a Branch shall grow out of his roots. And the Spirit of the Lord shall rest upon him, the spirit of wisdom and understanding, the spirit of counsel and might, the spirit of knowledge and of the fear of the Lord" (Isa. 11:1-2).

Furthermore, the prophet Isaiah summarizes the redeeming work of the Father, Son and Holy Spirit in the salvation of the lost as follows: "Behold my servant, whom I uphold; mine elect, in whom my soul delighteth; I have put my spirit upon him: he shall bring forth judgment to the Gentiles" (Isa. 42:1). Isaiah 61:1 reads: "The Spirit of the Lord God is upon me; because the Lord hath anointed me to preach good tidings unto the meek; he hath sent me to bind up the broken-hearted, to proclaim liberty to the captives, and the opening of the prison to them that are bound." Thus, in the New Testament, Jesus proclaims the fulfillment of this prophecy in Himself (Lk. 4:18-19). Furthermore, Christ as the risen and exalted Lord, is the Spirit. The Apostle John expresses it in this way: "But this spake he of the Spirit, which they that believe on him should receive: for the Holy Ghost was not yet given; because that Jesus was not yet glorified" (John 7:39). And so it is written, the first man Adam was made a living soul; and the last Adam was made a quickening Spirit (I Cor. 15:45). Hence, Christ as a life-giving Spirit desires to have fellowship with us in order for us to be transformed to the new image that He has obtained for us. Paul surmises that the ultimate goal of Christ becoming a life-giving Spirit is as follows: "And as we have borne the image of the earthy, we shall also bear the image of the heavenly" (I Cor. 15:49). "But we all, with open face beholding as in a glass the glory of the Lord, are changed into the same image from glory to glory, even as by the Spirit of the Lord" (II Cor. 3:18).

Similarly, the resurrection of our Lord and Saviour, Jesus Christ was a work of the Holy Trinity, Father, Son, and Holy Spirit. "For Christ hath once suffered for sins, the just for the unjust, that he might bring us to God, being put to death in the flesh but quickened by the Spirit" (I Pet, 3:18). "But if the Spirit of him that raised Jesus from the dead dwell in you, he that raised up Christ from the dead shall also quicken your mortal bodies by his Spirit that dwelleth in you. For as many as are lead by the Spirit of God, they are the sons of God" (Rom. 8:11, 14). And at the baptism of Jesus, we see the working in unity of the Trinity: When Jesus was baptized in the Jordan river, the Holy spirit descended upon Him like a dove and the Father spoke from heaven proclaiming that this is my beloved Son, in whom I am well pleased.

What is the Holy Spirit Like?

The Scriptures make apparent that the breath of God is the Spirit of God (Job 26:13); that God is a Spirit (invisible) and they that worship him must worship him in spirit and truth" (John 4:24). Furthermore, the Holy Spirit possesses all the essential characteristics of God: Omnipotence, or "all powerful" (Ps. 33:6); Omnipresence, or "everywhere present" (Ps. 139:7); and Omniscience, or "All knowing" (Ps.139:4). He is immutable which means that He is unchanging in character; He is the same yesterday, today and forevermore. Hence, the Holy Spirit is beyond time and space; He resides and abides in the heart and soul of every born-again Christian; and He is that part of God in us that is aware of and responsive to God. The Holy Spirit personally indwells the believer in Jesus Christ, thereby assuring our spiritual discernment. The Holy Spirit is our teacher, our Comforter, our Paraclete (the One by our side), and He is the Guide in our lives.

It is important for every individual to realize that the Holy Spirit is a person and because He is a person, He has a personality. The relevance of this knowledge as pertains to worship lies in the fact that each person must decide for oneself whether the Holy Spirit is truly the Spirit of God and a divine person who is worthy of our worship and adoration, our faith, our praise and our love. Similarly, as God the Father and God the Son are objects of prayer, so is the Holy Spirit an object of prayer. Moreover, the Holy Spirit was sent by the Father in answer to the prayer of the Son (John 14:16), for the purpose of drawing us to the Son. Therefore, the Holy Spirit assumes the awesome task of opening our blinded eyes, thereby allowing us to see our sinful condition, and then He reveals Jesus to us and enables us to accept Him as our Lord and Saviour. Therefore, the Holy Spirit organizes, illuminates, inspires, and sustains; He helps the saints in their weaknesses; He grants spiritual gifts, and He declares to the believer things that are to come.

The distinctive traits of personality ascribed to the Holy Spirit include knowledge, feelings and will. Since we know that the Holy Spirit is God and God is all knowing, we know also that The Holy Spirit has all knowledge (I Cor. 2:10, 11). Hence, the Holy Spirit has a mind, He can think and He has understanding (Eph. 1:17). The Scriptures ascribe "feelings of grief" to the Holy Spirit (Eph. 4:30) and makes reference to the "mind of the Spirit" (Rom. 8:27). Moreover, the word "mind" connotes the ideas of thought, feeling and purpose. Therefore, the Holy Spirit chooses, wills, convicts, acts and can be grieved. Finally, the Holy Spirit is a person of sovereign majesty who uses us according to His own will (I Cor. 12:11). However, since He is a gentleman, He does not force us against our will.

The Holy Spirit is an intercessor or one who prays. Likewise, the Spirit also helps our infirmities: for we know not what we should pray for as we ought, but the Spirit makes intercession for us with groanings which cannot be uttered. And He that searches the hearts knows the mind of the spirit, because He makes intercession for the saints according to the will of God (Rom. 8:26, 27). Moreover, not only does the Holy Spirit teach us and moves us to pray, but He also prays in us and through us. There is blessed assurance in the knowledge that every believer in Christ has two divine persons praying for us: God the Son and God the Holy Spirit. The Holy Spirit is our Teacher and our Comforter. The Apostle John writes: but when the Comforter, which is the Holy Ghost, whom the Father shall send in my name, He shall teach you all things, and bring all things to your remembrance, whatsoever I have said unto you (14:26). The means by which the Holy Spirit teaches us include suggestion, direction and illumination. Similarly, the Holy Spirit is represented as the "Spirit of Truth" as proclaimed by John: When He, the Spirit of truth is come, He will guide you to all truth (John 16:13). Hence, the Holy Spirit enables us not only to apprehend the truth of God, but He also leads, guides, and teaches us day-by-day. Therefore, the Holy Spirit teaches all believers the truths concerning the Scriptures and He leads and guides the children of God. For as many as are led by the Spirit of God, they are the sons of God (Rom. 8:14). Hence, the Holy Spirit is our present help; the person who takes us by the hand and gently leads us in the paths of righteousness all the days of our lives.

The Holy Spirit assumes the awesome task of indwelling, sealing, and sanctifying us and of helping us to be Christ-like in our character. Therefore, the Holy Spirit convicts, is active in believers, and is the cause of the believers salvation and sanctification. God predestined the believers' salvation through sanctification by the Spirit and through the belief of truth. Hence, Gentiles are made acceptable after being sanctified by the Holy Ghost (Rom. 15:16). The Holy Spirit regenerates and cleanses the hearts of true believers making them new beings in Christ Jesus. The Holy Spirit makes us aware of and reveals to us the abounding love that God has for His children. Through the Scriptures, we learn explicitly that God so loved the world that He gave His only begotten Son that whosoever believes on him should not perish but might have everlasting life. Likewise the Holy Spirit reveals to us who we are and whose we are: "Ye are of God, little children, and have overcome them: because greater is he that is in you, than he that is in the world" (I John 4:4). The Holy Spirit is that effective bond that unites believers to Christ, for He is the power of Christ in every believer that makes them know that He is theirs and they are His.

Very importantly, the Holy Spirit reveals to true believers the beauty of Christ's Holiness. For whom He foreknew, He also foreordained to be conformed to the image of His Son (Rom. 8:29). Just as Christ has redeemed us with his own precious blood, He also regenerates us through His Holy Spirit and conforms us to His own image. Hence, we are more than conquerors through Him that loved us (Rom. 8:37). And we know that all things work together for good to them that love God (Rom. 8:28). Our salvation, our being chosen for Christ was foreordained by God. He sent the Holy Spirit to lead us to Christ, and if we trust Him, He will lead us safely to our eternal home. The influence of the Holy Spirit in the Christian's life is manifested by the fruit of the Spirit, which is love, joy, peace, longsuffering, gentleness, goodness, faith, meekness, and temperance (Gal 5:22-23). For "if we live in the Spirit, let us also walk in the Spirit" (Gal. 5:25).

Numerous Scriptures emphasize that we had nothing to do with being chosen and we are not our own, we have been bought with a price. Jesus says: "Ye have not chosen me, but I have chosen you, and ordained you, that you should go and bring forth fruit, and that your fruit should remain: that whatsoever ye shall ask of the Father in my name, he may give it to you" (John 15:16). I have chosen you out of the world, therefore the world hates you (John 15:19). And Paul writes: "According as he has chosen us to Him before the foundation of the world, that we should be holy and without blame before Him in love. Having predestinated us unto the adoption of children by Jesus Christ to Himself, according to the good pleasure of His will. In whom we have redemption through His blood, the forgiveness of sins, according to the riches of His grace. That in the dispensation of the fullness of times, He might gather together in one all things in Christ, both which are in heaven, and which are on earth; even in Him" (Eph. 1:4-10). Because God has from the beginning chosen you to salvation through sanctification of the Spirit and belief of the truth (II Thes. 2:13).

The Holy Spirit makes known to believers the many promises and benefits that the Father has reserved for those who are righteous and faithful to the end. "For ye have need of patience, that, after ye have done the will of God, ye might receive the promise. *For yet a little while, and he that shall come will come, and will not tarry. Now the just shall live by faith: but if any man draw back, my soul shall have no pleasure in him* (Heb. 10:35-38). Moreover, The Holy Spirit gives the saints of God a foretaste of heaven. In Ephesians we read: "Blessed be the God and Father of our Lord Jesus Christ, who hath blessed us with all spiritual blessings in heavenly places in Christ. In whom ye also trusted, after that ye heard the word of truth, the gospel of your salvation: in whom also after ye believed, ye were sealed with that Holy Spirit of promise. Which is the earnest of our inheritance until the redemption of the purchased possession, unto the praise of his glory" (Eph 1:13-14). Hence, the Holy Spirit marks and seals believers forever and He gives them a foretaste of Christ's exceeding greatness — His Holiness, His Peace, His Rest, and His Love.

PART IV

EARTH'S FINAL CHAPTER

CHAPTER 12

THE ENIGMA OF DEATH

O Death, Where Is Thy Sting?
O Grave, Where Is Thy Victory?

— 1 Cor 15:55

Synopsis

This chapter conceptualizes life's journey as existing on a continuum from life to death to eternal life. The beginning of the chapter examines the various meanings and types of death: physical, spiritual, and eternal. Relevant scriptures which enhance one's understanding of the mystery of death are presented. The ending of the chapter discusses the reasons why the saints of God are blessed when they die and affirms that there is eternal blessedness to be enjoyed in the world to come after this life is ended.

The sting of death is sin; and the strength of sin is the law. But we give thanks to our God, who gives us the victory through our Lord and Savior Jesus Christ (I Cor.15:55-57). Therefore, over both law and sin, God has given us the victory. Through the shed blood of Jesus Christ, the law's curse and sin's condemnation are removed. We are dead to the law by the body of Christ (Rom. 7:14). Death's dominion is ended, although its power to kill the most Holy Body, and to detain the most sacred dust for a short time is not taken away. In other words, the Grace of Christ has made sin a broken enemy, the law a friend and death a useful servant.

Thanks be to God!!! To the Father, Son and Holy Spirit, our One God, be all Holy Obedience!!! Laws bind to Obedience, and Benefits unto Thankfulness. But God, who is our Law-giver is in all things and is, also, our Benefactor. All of His Laws are Benefits, and we owe to Him all Obedient Thankfulness, and all Thankful Obedience! We owe our all to Him "Who gives us the victory, through our Lord Jesus Christ. His Gift of Grace is given to Believers Only!! The Lord, Jesus Christ is the purchaser of it; whose death gave the Angel of Death his mortal wound and whose Resurrection has certified and exemplified Believers! His Righteousness, by Faith received, bestows on Believers the power of Everlasting Life. The Sanctifying Spirit of our Lord Jesus Christ mortifies sinful lusts, which is a sting of death. His Comforting Spirit takes away the pain and anguish that sin sticks in our souls.

Moreover, we can say of death and all enemies in combination with it, that whosoever is born of God, overcomes the world: and this is the victory that overcomes the world, even our faith. And it is he who believes in the Son of God that overcomes the world (I Jn. 5:4-5). Jesus Christ has abolished death and brought life and immortality to light through the gospel (II Tim.1:10). Believers can truly rejoice in their victory over death. And the good news is that Christ arose, breaking the bonds of death and leaving an empty grave. Indeed, death has been defeated and the door to eternal life has been opened to believers. Therefore, victory over death is certainly the most desired, and obtained good of Believers. And the Holy Ghost, the Comforter is expressly named a Witness to Believers of their being taken into the number and being blessed with all the privileges of the Sons of God.

Although the subject of death is discussed extensively in the Scriptures, it remains a hidden mystery or an enigma, to the human mind. The Bible describes the deaths of many Old and New Testament personalities and makes clear the inevitability of death. In all of human history, only Enoch and Elijah did not die. Hence, Hebrews 9:27 tells us: "It is appointed unto men once to die, but after this the judgment." Believers should not fear or dread death, because you the Lord has blessed! God has called you out of darkness! God has loosed you from the captivity of Satan! God has allowed you to experience His Goodness in the Light and Life of His Son Jesus Christ! Therefore, Christians can face death fearlessly because Christ has conquered death (I Cor. 15:55-57). I suppose the most frightening aspect of death is not knowing what happens to a person after one dies. In growing up, most of us have heard many myths about whether there is or is not life after death. And there are many people who believe that life ends at the grave. Moreover, the unsaved do not seek salvation and die in their sins, because they have not learned of God's redemption plan for mankind which was executed by Christ on the cross, giving the saved life everlasting.

In April 1985, my son died tragically in a motorcycle accident and two months later, my mother died of a stroke and heart attack. Because I was incapable, at that time, of perceiving of death beyond the physical realm, death became my most feared enemy. I did not understand why they had to die; all I knew was that two significant people in my life had been suddenly taken away from me, and I did not know what to do. I began to search the Scriptures for answers; I cried out to God to help me to understand my confused life; and I asked Him to give me the strength that I needed to make it through what I was going through.

The first thing that I learned from my study is that death is not the end of life, but the separation of the body from the spirit. The Bible teaches us that we are more than physical beings; we are also spiritual beings. Therefore, for humans, physical death does not mean the end of existence but the end of life as we know it and the transition to another dimension in which our conscious existence continues. Since man's existence is three-fold; body, soul and spirit; death can also be conceptualized in a three-fold manner: physical, spiritual and eternal. Moreover, when a person dies, it is not that end of life itself; but it is the separation of the body from the spirit. The body and soul return to the dust and the spirit goes back to God.

The first death of a human being recorded in the Bible is that of Abel who was murdered by his brother Cain (Gen. 4:8). However, death is first mentioned by God Himself: "But of the tree of the knowledge of good and evil, thou shalt not eat of it: for in the day that you eat thereof you shall surely die" (Gen. 2:17). Likewise, the

Apostle Paul speaks of death as an enemy: "The last enemy that will be destroyed is death" (I Cor. 15:26). Moreover, in His death, burial and resurrection, Jesus conquered death: physical, spiritual and eternal. Through fear of death people are subject to bondage (Heb. 2:15). But our Lord and Saviour, Jesus Christ has abolished death, and has brought life and immortality to light through the Gospel (II Tim. 1:10). Jesus said: "I am come that they might have life, and that they might have it more abundantly" (John 10:10). "I am the resurrection, and life: he that believes in me, though he were dead, yet shall he live: And whosoever lives and believes in me shall never die" (John 11:25, 26). Likewise, Paul writes in Ephesians that you were dead in trespasses and sins, and God has quickened you and has raised us up together, and made us sit together in heavenly places in Christ Jesus (Eph.2:1,6). Therefore, God has reconciled His people unto Himself and has given them life in abundance.

God created people to live forever, both physically and spiritually. However, because of one man's disobedience, death became everyone's lot: "Wherefore, as by one man sin entered into the world, and death by sin; and so death passed upon all men" (Rom. 5:12). The Bible speaks of both types of death; that is the death of the saved and the unsaved. Those who are outside of Christ are alive physically, but they are spiritually dead, that is, "dead in trespasses and sins" (Eph. 2:1). Since in physical death, the spirit is separated from the body, the believer's spirit goes to Paradise, which is a special place in Heaven prepared by Christ for the saints. When Jesus was crucified on the cross between two thieves, one of the thieves said to Jesus: "Lord remember me when you come into your kingdom" (Luke 23:42). And Jesus said unto him, "Assuredly, I say to you, today you will be with me in Paradise" (verse 43). Those who are outside of Christ are alive physically, but they are dead spiritually. And if they persist in their unbelief, they shall remain forever in spiritual death; that is in eternal separation from God. The book of Revelation refers to eternal damnation as the second death (21:8). It is called the second death, not because existence or consciousness ends, but because it pronounces eternal separation from the presence of God.

I have chosen to conceptualize life as existing on a continuum: Physical Birth → Physical Growth & Development → Rebirth

(Spiritual Regeneration) → Sanctification & Holiness → Spiritual, Physical, Mental & Emotional Maturity → Physical Decline → Spiritual Rejuvenation → Physical Death → Eternal Life (Everlasting Life)

I believe that when we can perceive of life and death as a dynamic process on a continuum, then we can more readily accept death as a necessary stage in our progression from mortal life to eternal life. The diagram which I have just described is a depiction of this concept. Life is transitory — We do not know what will happen tomorrow, nor for that matter when we will die. But we do know that as sure as you are born, you shall die. There is an abundance of Scriptures that make this truth clear. For what is your life? It is only a mist that appears for a little while and then vanishes (James 4:14). Moreover, we must accept that our life is but a breath. When the breath leaves the body, the body is dead. If we want to make the most of our lives, we must face the fact that it will someday end. We may argue, bargain, plead, or negotiate, but one thing is certain, we must accept the truth that death is a universal enemy that each of us must face.

The Bible stresses that death is an enemy of both God and man. The Apostle Paul writes: "For He must reign, until He has put all his enemies under His feet. The last enemy that shall be destroyed is death" (I Cor. 15:25 - 26). Why is death an enemy of God? The answer is simply because death destroys life, in contrast to God, who is the creator and giver of life. In fact, the Bible makes clear that neither sin nor pain, sickness or death were a part of God's original plan for man. God created man and woman as perfect beings who were to live with Him forever in Paradise. Death became a penalty for Adam and Eve's sin, who of their own free will chose to disobey God. God had told them that if they ate of the tree of knowledge of good and evil, they would die (Gen. 2:17). Adam and Eve chose to disobey God's instructions and to believe Satan's lie, "you shall not surely die" (Gen. 3:4).

Adam was created in innocence, which means "void of sin," but because Adam disobeyed God, sin entered the world through him. Moreover, death became the penalty for sin and man was taken out of eternity and placed in time (Gen.3:22) Hence, the Apostle Paul writes: "Wherefore, as by one man sin entered into the world, and death by sin; and so death passed upon all men, for all have sinned" (Rom. 5:12). Further, he states, "For the wages of sin is death; but the gift of God is eternal life through Jesus Christ our Lord" (Rom. 6:23)

Why Lord? Why Lord? Why Lord?

Sometimes the mysterious dealings of the Lord may cause the believer to complain to God and even to ask him why? I suppose the most painful circumstance that cause Christians to question the rationale of God's actions are situations that involve loss. We experience loss any time we have to part from or lose someone or something that was once ours and that we hold dear in our hearts and lives.

Now, there are some religiously pious persons who will tell you that you should never question God; that to question God is indicative of a lack of faith. And so, by their reasoning, you should not ask God why? — under any circumstances! — even when you lose your job and maybe your home! — even when you end up in a shelter or, worse, on the streets! They advocate that you should not ask God "why me?" — when your health fails and you lose an organ or body part, — or when your heart, liver or kidneys fail! Further, they say don't ask "why my child?" when your child dies in an accident, is killed, or dies from an acute illness or a chronic disease! And when you have cried out in earnest to God, they even go so far as to say that you should not ask, "Why Lord are you not answering me?" They suggest that you should not go to the only One who has the power to help you bear the burden that you are carrying — the only burden bearer, the only heavy load carrier.

Now the problem with this philosophical viewpoint is that it is not found in the Word of God. As a matter of fact, the Bible is replete with demonstrations of God's desire that we cry out to Him in our attempts to understand His purpose and plans for our lives. The Bible tells us to cast our burden upon the Lord, and He shall sustain us (Ps. 55:22). The book of Habakkuk gives a striking example of a prophet who cried out to God concerning problems of human suffering and evil that he saw and challenged God's plan to judge the nation of Judah by the pagan Babylonians (Hab.1:12 - 2:1). Finally, his deep faith inspired him to write a poem of praise in response to the mysterious ways of God (Hab. 3). In the first two chapters of the book, Habakkuk protests, complains, and questions God about His actions. This Scripture, quite vividly, illustrates the experience of a godly person's strivings to comprehend the confused issues around him and he cries out to the Lord. He sobs his complaint to God: "O Lord, how long shall I cry, and you will not hear! even cry out unto you of violence, and you will not save! Why do you show me iniquity and cause me to behold grievance" (Hab.1:1-3).

The historical account of Habakkuk's dilemma is instructive of the spiritual decline, the crime, violence, and idol worship in Judah, and the imminent invasion of Jerusalem. Likewise, the question and answer technique of the prophet Habakkuk teaches a valuable lesson about the nature of God. The fact that God allows Himself to be questioned by one of His followers is an indication of His Grace! Kindness! and Tender Mercy! which He freely gives to His children. In his deep perplexity, Habakkuk could not comprehend how a Holy and Righteous God could allow the wicked to prosper, while things were going from bad to worse in Judah. He wonders why God is allowing these things to happen. His doubts increased as he tries to reconcile a Good God and righteous laws with the rampant evil that abounded in the land. Habakkuk could not dismiss his doubts without an answer and so he cries out: "O Lord how long shall I cry and you will not hear!"

There is no doubt in my mind that Habakkuk was God-fearing and his refusal to be turned off by what he saw was born out of a deep faith in the power and providence of a Holy and Righteous God. Habakkuk could not understand how God could use a pagan force to punish Judah and so he challenges God to defend His actions. Moreover, reverently and expectantly, Habakkuk seeks an answer from the Lord. "I will stand upon my watch, and set me upon the tower, and will watch to see what He will say unto me, and what I shall answer when I am reproved" (Hab. 2:1).

There is a great lesson in this passage for all of us. After Habakkuk had cried out to God, he goes up to the watchtower to await the answer. Although the scripture does not tell us how long he waited, it does lead us to believe that we too must wait for an answer. And implicit in all of this is the realization that God will answer in His own time and way, and not in ours. The answer may seem slow in coming, but believers know that God will work out all the dilemmas in our lives for our good and for His glory. The Apostle Paul tells us that all things work together for good for those who love God, to them who are the called according to His purpose(Rom. 8:28).

The importance of waiting on God is also emphasized by Isaiah who states: "Those who wait on the Lord shall renew their strength; they shall mount up with wings as eagles; they shall run, and not be weary; and they shall walk and not faint" (Is.40:31). We can shout hallelujah to our God, because grieving believers have learned that in God's favor is life: weeping may endure for a night, but joy comes in the morning (Ps. 30:5). The eye of the Lord is upon them that fear Him, upon them that hope in His mercy; to deliver their soul from death. That's why our soul waits on the Lord, He is our help, our shield and our God (Ps.33:18 - 20).

Hence, the story of Job reassures us that questioning God is common to the human experience. In his sorrow, he sits mourning in ashes and laments his misfortune. His three friends who came to mourn with him and to offer their comfort did not do this; instead they launch a debate to show the reason for Job's suffering. Their discourses were reflective of the prevailing line of thought that misfortune is sent by God as punishment for sin. Job argues that he has done nothing to deserve such treatment at the hand of God and he asks God why? why? why? Yet in all their debates, they were not able to come up with a satisfactory solution. God did not enter into their discussion about why the righteous suffer; instead, He answered Job out of a whirlwind and reveals Himself as the powerful, all-knowing God. His message to Job, and to the rest of us for that matter, is that He does not have to explain or justify His actions. He is the sovereign, all-powerful God who always does what is right, although His ways may be beyond human understanding. He does not have to explain Himself, nor is He required to reveal His grand design. He reveals Himself and His plans, in His own way and in His own time.

Job is thoroughly humbled by this outpouring of God's power, and he learns to trust where he cannot understand. This leads to Job's great affirmation of faith: "I have uttered what I did not understand, things too wonderful for me, which I did not know" (42:3). "I have heard of You by the hearing of the ear, but now my eye sees You" (42:5). And the Bible says that "The Lord blessed Job's latter end more than his beginning" (42:12). And what about us? We must learn to trust God at all times, everywhere, in everything, in every situation, in every circumstance — even when we don't understand why! This is where our faith becomes evident! You see, faith is being sure of what we believe God will do and certain of what we do not see. In other words, faith is taking God at His Word. God's Word tells us to not look at things which are seen; for the things which are seen are temporal but the things which are not seen are eternal (II Cor. 4:18). But without faith it is impossible to please God. Any one who comes to God must believe that "He is, and that He is a rewarder of them that diligently seek Him (Heb. 11:6)."

We ponder, and even books have been written about "Why bad things happen to good people"? The answer lies in the Sovereignty of God. In His Sovereignty, God can do what He wants to, when He wants to, how He wants to and why He wants to. He doesn't have to ask our permission!!! Furthermore, God has not promised us only sunshine, but a little rain mixed with the sunshine and also a little pain.

I remember when my son died, I prayed earnestly to God and asked him to give my son back to me. I knew that He could do it because He had raised Lazarus from the grave after he had laid there for four long days (Jn.11:43). Not only did I know that He could do it, I believed that He would do it. And, He did not. Although God did not give my son back, He did give me a confirmation that Eric was sleeping with the Lord. In a dream, Eric and I were going through the cafeteria line on my job, when suddenly we were caught up in a cloud. Then a hand reached out from the cloud to Eric and a voice said, "you come with me." And the voice said to me, " but you go back, you're not ready yet." Initially, I thought that this referred to my salvation; but later I came to realize that God sent me back because He had a special work for me to do in ministering to bereaved and other hurting people through my writing, preaching, and teaching.

Herein lies a critical lesson about faith. And so we ask "what is faith." For many people faith is equated with victory. When we pray and God gives us what we prayed for, we believe and others believe with us, as well. The lesson to be learned here is that faith has nothing to do with victory. Faith is not a response to evidence, even when that evidence is clearly miraculous. Your faith can never be based on what is done in the natural, but rather, it must be based on what happens in the spiritual. Let me make it clear for you. You see, a person realizes faith and the power of faith by knowing the source of faith. And that Source is Jesus Christ. Praise God!!!

CHAPTER 13

UNDERSTANDING GRIEF
AND MOURNING

Synopsis

Chapter thirteen defines grief and mourning within the context of death and the afterlife. It explains the processes of grief and mourning, and discusses specific coping strategies which lead to positive adjustment to the loss of a loved one. Finally, this chapter discusses some commonly experienced emotions related to grief and mourning, and lists some healthy measures for adapting to the changes in one's life.

Additionally, chapter thirteen provides a portrayal of the natural phenomena of conception and childbirth. Within the context of biblical history, the author discusses mothers' who have either grieved the death of a child, or have grieved their inability to have a child. The last part of the chapter is therapeutic in focus and seeks to counsel and encourage not only bereaved mothers and others who mourn; but also to acquaint women and men everywhere with Jesus the Christ and to bring salvation to the unsaved.

I don't know whether understanding is an appropriate term for what we as finite human beings are seeking when a loved one dies. We ask the question why? And as we ponder in our minds and mourn in our hearts, we search here and there for the answer. The critical work that must be done in mourning is not in understanding why our loved one has died, but in facing the reality of what has occurred. This is important because if, on the one hand, you get caught up in the why, you avoid the fact that your loved one has died. On the other hand, by facing the "that," you also deal with the "why." We may never know why on a physical, emotional or spiritual level. Therefore, we must put aside the discussion of why our loved one died, and face the reality that they have died.

Some psychologists view grief as an emotion involving our affect or feelings. This viewpoint suggests that the emotion of grief is a complex experience wrought out of our feelings relative to the pain and anguish associated with loss. Although objectively and rationally, we must face the reality of death, and yet societally, we must behave as though the loss has not occurred. And so the dilemma becomes one of reconciling the real state with the perceived state. This process, which we refer to as grieving or mourning, presents a wide array of symptoms and feelings and is an important part of healing.

The word grief is a general term used to describe an emotional state or condition caused by a loss from whatever the source. Whereas, bereavement is a more specific term used to describe an emotional state or condition caused by death. Specifically, grieving is the process employed in response to a loss from any source and mourning relates to the coping responses that one employs when a loved one dies.

Death is a very stressful event that impacts each of our lives differently and the methods we use in coping are, in large part, based on how we have coped with the stresses of life in the past. For example, persons who have faced stressful situations in the past by facing the problem and developing strategies to move forward will more than likely approach death in this same way. By contrast, persons who have had problems in coping with stress will possibly have difficulties adjusting to the death of a loved one. Adjustment is a process that is used to accommodate changes in one's normal life pattern. Any loss is disruptive of one's pattern of functioning and, therefore, requires decisions about how one will function in the changed state. Moreover, as we grieve or mourn, we behave in ways that are individualized and characteristically our own. No one can tell you how you should or should not adjust to a loss in your life.

Again, how we mourn is an individual matter and varies from one person to another. However, there are some common aspects to the normal mourning process that I would like to mention. God placed inside of man a soul which is the seat of our emotions or feelings. Some theorists refer to this faculty as affections of the heart. The emotions are a major factor in grief. Within our emotional make-up, we find contrary or contrasting feelings — some examples are: love vs. hate, joy vs. sorrow, happy vs. sad, and hope vs. despair. Anger is an affection of the heart that seems to be a mixture of sorrow and hatred. Sadness is an obvious emotion experienced by bereaved persons. The sad countenance (sad facial expression) and ashen grey complexion are obvious signs of this emotion.

Some of the commonly experienced emotions during bereavement or mourning include denial, guilt, anxiety, and depression.

1. Denial is the body's response to protect the mind and involves an avoidance of reality and a denial of what has happened.

2. Guilt feelings relate to the blaming of oneself for the persons death and feeling that the death is punishment for something one did or something one failed to do.

3. Anxiety is an overwhelming sense of apprehension and fear, usually accompanied by rapid pulse and shallow rapid breathing. Anxiety attacks are not at all uncommon and are brought on by hyperventilation.

4   Depression is a mental state of extreme sadness which is characterized by an increase or decrease in appetite and sleep patterns, feelings of hopelessness, and sometimes suicidal tendencies.

Mourning is not solely an emotional response. The bereaved can experience physical symptoms, such as headaches, digestive disturbances, change in appetite, weight gain or loss, sleep disturbances, sexual difficulties, lack of energy, inability to concentrate, rapid heart rate, and breathing difficulties.

Taking care of the body is very important to the mourning process because healing of the emotions cannot occur in an unhealthy body. Some of the things that you can do to promote natural healing include the following:

1. Get adequate rest and maintain proper nutrition.

2. Avoid stimulants such as caffeine and nicotine and depressants such as alcohol.

3. Practice relaxation and deep breathing exercises.

4. Exercise moderately and take relaxing walks.

5. Give yourself permission to grieve and cry; crying is healing.

6. Seek professional help if you are unable to grieve, if your physical symptoms seem to be getting worse, and/or if you are engaged in some kind of self-destructive behavior. Do not take medication except under the supervision of a physician or other licensed professional.

The Grieving Mother

God has given mothers a very special affection of the heart which is called a "Mother's love." This affection grows out of an innate instinct or maternal drive which means to nourish and protect. This instinct which God has given only to mothers creates a special bond between mother and baby that does not exist naturally in any other relationship. This special bond develops out of nine months in which the mother carries her baby and he grows and develops inside of her. They are attached to a common blood and air line, and a common food and water line, which is established through the umbilical cord and a special organ called the placenta. Now if you will allow me to, I will break this down for you. In simple terms, the baby eats what the mother eats, drinks what the mother drinks, and ingests or inhales what the mother ingests or inhales. In other words, for nine months, mother and baby are one.

At birth, the placenta detaches itself from the mother's womb and the umbilical cord is cut. And now, the baby must breathe, take in nourishment and eliminate wastes on his own. The place where the placenta detaches is now an open wound with bleeding. Through the body's natural defenses, the wound gradually heals and the mother's womb goes back to its normal position and size. The mother is encouraged to follow good health practices because they promote the healing process.

Historically, women have grieved either their inability to bear a child, or over the loss of a child that they had born. Eve was the first woman, the first wife, and the first mother to bury a child. The Biblical examples of how God will restore what you have lost are numerous. God gave Eve another son called Seth or "appointed." "For God," said she "has appointed me another seed instead of Abel, whom Cain slew" (Gen. 4:25).

Naomi buried her husband and ten years later buried her two married sons. The story of Naomi and her daughter-in-law, Ruth, is a beautiful story of love and loyalty. Ruth was a Gentile, and a virtuous woman who chose the God of the Hebrews to be her God. She was the mother of Obed and the grandmother of David, placing her in the direct genealogy of Jesus the Christ. And Naomi in her old age was blessed by the Lord because through Ruth, Naomi was given a son that his name might be famous in Israel (Ruth 4:14).

Hannah was the fourth great woman in the Bible who grieved because she had not conceived. Hannah took her problem to God and depended on him for a child. She attempted to overcome her grief by going to the temple and praying. She prayed for a son and made a vow or promise to the Lord that if He would give her a male child, she would give him back to the Lord all the days of his life (I Sam. 1:11).

Hannah gave birth to a son and named him Samuel, meaning "asked of the Lord." When Samuel was weaned, Hannah kept her promise and took him to the temple and left him in the hands of Eli, the priest. Because of her faithfulness, God blessed her with three sons and two daughters (I Sam. 2:21). When we pray as Hannah prayed, we must know that God answers in His own way and at His own set time.

When we place what we have in the Master's hands, He multiplies and magnifies it into an abundance. For He is able to do exceeding abundantly above all that we ask or think, according to His mighty power that works in us (Eph. 3:20).

Mary, the mother of Jesus grieved the death of her first born son. Her deepest agony and greatest sorrow occurred as she stood at the Cross of Calvary and witnessed the crucifixion of Jesus (John 19:25). Simeon had prophesied to Mary that she would have great sorrow because of what would happen to Jesus. The essence of his prophecy is found in Luke 2; 35: "(Yea, a sword shall pierce through thy own soul also,) that the thoughts of many hearts may be revealed." Mary kept all these things and pondered them in her heart.

Faith and trust in the Lord Jesus will sustain us in our grief; however, unbelief hinders us from being able to experience God's amazing grace. Trust in our environment develops out of loving and caring relationships with significant people in our lives. The Christian's trust in God develops out of intimate relationships with our Lord and Savior, Jesus Christ.

A frequent emotion experienced by parents is guilt. Guilt feelings escalate as the enemy, who is the accuser of God's people, continually reminds you of your past and tells you that your child died because of your sins. Satan tries to confuse you by distorting your knowledge of God and His plans for your life. Likewise, you can expect the enemy to try to distract you by trying to block or hold-up the message that God is sending you. Satan is relentless in his attacks, he tries to tire you out, cloud your spiritual vision, and plants lies about you whenever he can. I remember when my son died, I relived every sin in my past, even those in my childhood. Satan reminded me of every bad thing that I had ever done and by the time he finished with me, I felt like the worst kind of sinner and I truly believed that I was just getting what I deserved.

Well, I want you to know that Satan always operates in a very deceitful way. He will use anybody or anything that he can to confuse you, to kill your spirit and destroy you. Now, the reason I know that Satan sends his followers to confuse you is because of what happened to me a couple days after my son's death. That morning, two Jehovah witnesses appeared at my door. In my grief, I hysterically told them about my son's motorcycle accident and death. They told me that they had read about my son in the newspapers and the tragic way that he had died. Then they asked me, "what kind of God are you serving that would kill your son that way?" I very quickly asked them to leave, closed my door and called my pastor. My late pastor explained to me that this was a trick of the enemy. He listened to me, encouraged me, and prayed for me. The late Dr. George B. Rogers was my greatest support and although he was well in his eighties, I knew God had kept him here for me and my family.

Often people with perfectly good intentions will say to you "I know how you feel" or "I know what you are going through." And they will sometimes add, I remember "when mother died," or "when my husband died," or "when aunt Sallie died." Please understand that it is not my intention to minimize the pain of losing any significant person in one's life; but it is my desire that you will understand that the death of one's child is very different from any other loss. I believe that the most painful experience that any parent will have to endure is to bury your child. No other person comes from you, except your child. Your child is bone of your bones and flesh of your flesh, because your child comes from you. I do not believe that anyone who has not had a child die can know or fully understand what the pain of losing a child really feels like. In your mind, you can imagine what it might feel like, but you cannot know.

Then there are those who will attempt to equate the depth of your grief with the age of the deceased child. Your child is your child at any age. Should you grieve less if your child dies at twenty or thirty, as opposed to two or three, or as a newborn. "No, indeed not!" The death of a child at any age produces a torrent, or outpouring, of emotions and an indescribable void or emptiness on the inside. There is intense sorrow, sadness, helplessness, extreme emotional distress, anger, guilt, and an excruciating pain, that seemingly will not go away.

When a child dies, it does not matter what the age of the child might be: stillborn, premature, infant, young child, teenager, young adult, or adult; for the mother, the birth of her child is recreated in her mind. She experiences a hollowness, intense pain and an emptiness inside of her that she can not touch or describe, and that will not go away. The magnitude of shock is so powerful that it blocks out one's ability to feel, and a numbness sets in. This is a defense mechanism to protect the psyche. Initially, the fragile mind may not be able to face the reality of the loss, and thus cannot move forward. After the initial periods of grief, the mourning process goes on for many months and years afterwards. God gave us a natural ability to heal, but it takes time for this healing process to occur.

We cannot underestimate the difficulty that bereaved parents face in trying to cope and ultimately adjust their lives to the loss of a child. The pain associated with the death of a child is enormously destructive to one's life and family. Physical, psychological, emotional, social, and spiritual maladaptations are quite common. Seemingly, there is no comfort and no consolation. The despair and torment devastates bereaved parents who pray for relief from the unbearable pain and emptiness on the inside. Some mourners become physically exhausted and lack the energy for even daily activities of living. Still others feel varying degrees of anxiety, helplessness, hopelessness, and powerlessness.

Some parents go through a period of bargaining, — with anyone, — with God — with the devil. "I'll trade you anything for my child's life." But none of this is to any avail and many parents become very angry with God for taking their child away. They are also angry with all the people who said all the wrong things when the child died and all those who criticized the parent's reaction in their grief. Some parents believe that the grief of bereaved parents is indescribable and, therefore, cannot adequately be put in words. Furthermore, there are a few parents who no not believe that "time heals all wounds." As previously stated, each person's grief experience is individualized and may be different. For me, time has eased the pain, time has made things better, and time has healed the wounds. But it has left scars that I have had to learn to live with. Granted, time does not make the pain go away completely, but it does lessen the pain, so that it does not hurt with the same intensity. Although the pain is still there and it is real indeed; it doesn't hurt as badly as it once did, because you learn to control it. This means that you must learn to take one day at a time, for the rest of your life. Since there is nothing that you can do to bring your child back, you must get on with your life and continue living.

In coping with the grief of losing a child, the first thing that parents must do is to give yourself permission and then take the time to grieve. Parents need to have someone to listen to them and understand their problem. This is an especially critical time when you need someone who will listen to you and not judge you and who will allow you to share your pain and memories of your loved one. You should write down your feelings and, most importantly, you need to seek spiritual guidance. Faith in God will sustain you and help you in coping with your bereavement. You can depend on the promises of God in Scripture, both pertaining to life after death for believers and help for you in your grief. It is not uncommon for parents to feel that they have nothing to live for. However, you may feel assured that the pain will lessen and a sense of purpose and meaning will return in your life.

Parents are very vulnerable at this time and should think seriously about whether they need grief counseling. Many times parents just need to verify that they are not crazy. Counseling may be necessary when there is no family member or friend to talk to and who will help you go through the pain. Mourning should never be done totally alone. Also, if there are serious emotional problems that do not allow the grieving process to take place; grief counseling should be sought. Some way, some how, effective mourning must take place and this process takes time, from many months to many years. Bereaved persons have to go on living, for themselves, their family and the people around them. Finally, I must caution mourners that there are real dangers in healing too fast or too soon. As strange as this may sound, there can be dreadful problems with getting well too quickly. It's like the scar on a wound that may heal on the outside, but inside is festering. Many times what appears on the surface to be a parent healing amazingly fast will emerge later in tragic ways. My advice is that your mourn, with the help of the Holy Spirit, in your own way and in your own time.

PART V

A GLIMPSE OF HEAVEN

CHAPTER 14

THE CHRISTIAN'S VIEWPOINT
OF HEAVEN

Synopsis

A glimpse of heaven emphasizes that heaven is a place of fulfillment in God where the saints live eternally in the presence of God. The portrayal of mansions in heaven by Jesus Christ, the viewpoint of heaven of the Apostle Paul, and the visions of heaven written in the book of Revelation by the Apostle John are briefly examined and interpreted. Scriptures that substantiate that there is life after death and that there is a heaven and a hell are presented. In graphic detail, the book of Revelation places the redeemed around the heavenly throne occupied by God, Jesus Christ, angels, and a cloud of witnesses. The Apostle John envisions the next life as everlasting worship of God.

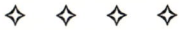

For many centuries, the question of whether heaven is symbolic or literal has been extensively debated. Various Scriptures which presumably support both positions can be found throughout the Bible. In like manner, the question of what happens after death continues to be as perplexing and pressing as it was in the early Christian era. This chapter will survey scriptural connotations relative to heaven and life after death.

The term "heaven" refers primarily to the sky above us, which serves as the firmament to which the stars are attached, and the pair "heaven and earth" or the triad "heaven, earth or sea" represents the entire created universe. Heaven is the dwelling place of God (Gen.28:17; Rev.12:10). It is called the Father's house because it is the place where God and his heavenly family reside(Jn. 14:1-3). The word "heaven" is also used as a substitute for the name of God (Luke 15:18, 21; Jn. 3:27). The kingdom of God and the Kingdom of heaven are often spoken of interchangeably in scripture (Matt. 4:17; Mk.1:15). Moreover, the New Testament perspective on heaven and eternal life was shaped by two main foci: The first focus was directed toward God and having an intimate relationship with the divine. And the second was related to the rejection of kinship, marriage, and earthly or fleshly concerns.

For the Christian viewpoint of heaven is that it is the "place" where the righteous will spend eternity when this life is ended. In the New Testament, the Messianic kingdom becomes the kingdom of heaven or the heavenly kingdom (II Tim.. 4:18), where our proper common-wealth is (Phil. 3:20). Our reward is in heaven (Matt. 5:12; Lk. 6:23), and it is in heaven that we are to store up treasures which are not subject to the losses to which the treasures of the world are exposed (Matt.6:20; Lk 12:33). Our physical body or earthly tabernacle will be dissolved and replaced by an eternal home in heaven (II Cor.5:1). The Bible says that Christians can rejoice because their names are written in heaven (Lk.10:20). The Christian life with God begins by symboli-cally putting off the old garment in baptism and accepting a new life in Christ (Mk.16:16). Total renewal is attained only when the old garment, or physical body, is replaced with a new resurrection body, or spiritual body, in heaven.

For the Christian, the greatest of all joys relates to being delivered from the tribulations of this world and living forever with God. This marvelous feat has been made possible for believers through the saving work of Jesus Christ. Since Jesus rose from the dead and was glorified by ascending into heaven, our salvation assures us that if we die with Him, we shall also live with Him, and if we endure, we shall also reign with Him (II Tim.2:8, 10-12). Jesus said: "And I, if I be lifted up from the earth, will draw all men unto me" (Jn. 12:32). Jesus is the way, the truth, and the life and He is the only way to the Father

(Jn.14:6). Hence, the life of the Christian on earth is but a journey toward their heavenly home and eternal resting place.

The belief in life after death is quite universal, not only in this present age, but in ages past and throughout history. Therefore, Job asks this universal question: "If a man dies, shall he live again?" (14:14). Likewise in the book of the beginnings, Eve ponderers the same question as she listened to the serpent's lie "Ye shall not surely die" (Gen.3:4). Hence, we are reminded that to everything there is a season, and a time to every purpose under the heaven: a time to be born and a time to die (Eccl.3:1-2). Many earlier writers viewed life after death in terms of the re-establishment of the Jewish state or as a special reward for the virtuous. However in the New Testament viewpoint, heaven is not the place where those who lacked something would find fulfillment, but rather it is the promise that Christians would have the blessed assurance of being in the present of God throughout all of eternity.

CHAPTER 15

JESUS CHRIST'S PROMISE OF EVERLASTING LIFE

Synopsis

This chapter stresses that Jesus Christ is the chief architect of the new image of heaven. It explains the meaning of Paradise, a place where believer's in Christ will rest from their labors and wait for their rewards. The chapter gives several portrayals of Jesus' God-centered, anti-family perspective of heaven.

Early Christian teachings emphasized that God rewarded the good, either on a renewed earth or in a blessed heaven. Therefore, Christians looked forward to life in the next world, where there would no longer be darkness, but the light of God would brighten their way throughout all of eternity. Moreover, an array of apocalyptic teachings stressed the resurrection of the dead, God's final judgment, and the establishment of an everlasting divine kingdom.

Jesus Christ is the chief architect of the new image of heaven, however, there are some important expansions and modifications which were made by the Apostle Paul writing in the New Testament epistles, and the Apostle John writing in the book of Revelation. In spite of some minor differences in focus, it is important to note that all three viewpoints stress the importance of a personal relationship with God through Jesus Christ in order to achieve the promised everlasting blessedness. The New Testament promise of eternal life stresses leaving the limitations of this life in the grave and spending eternity in the presence of God.

The Bible says that Jesus was crucified on a cross in a place called Calvary between two thieves. The thief on the right said to Jesus "Lord remember me when you come into your kingdom." And Jesus said to him "Assuredly I say to you, today you will be with me in Paradise (Lk.23:32-33, 42-43)." Jesus created Paradise as a place in heaven where believer's in Christ will rest from their labors and wait for their rewards. The kingdom of God or the kingdom of heaven has already arrived with the first coming of Christ (Matt.12:28; Lk.17:20-21) and His second coming is still awaited (Rev. 22:12).

Jesus describes His Father's house or heaven as having many mansions. This means that there are many individual rooms or dwelling places in God's house. In heaven believers will live in one place with the Father, the Son, and all other believers throughout the ages. Furthermore, Jesus promised that He would go and prepare a place for us, and then He will come again and receive us unto Himself; so that where He is, we may be also. We must realize the importance of our salvation, because the only way that we can spend eternity with God is through His Son, Jesus Christ. Jesus said: "I am the way, the truth, and the life: no man comes to the Father, but by me" (Jn. 14:2-3, 6).

Although Jesus Christ did not leave a written legacy of Himself, we are able to study His life through the Four Gospels. The gospel passages pertaining to heaven reveal not only Jesus' perspective on heaven as a place; but also on life after death or what is known as the afterlife. Through several gospel passages, we are able to view the scenario presented to Jesus by the Sadducees (Matt.22:23-28; Mk.12:18-23; Lk.20:27-33). The Bible says that the scenario presented to Christ was as follows: If a man's brother dies, leaving a wife and no children, the law of Moses says that the brother should marry the widow and raise their children for his dead brother. Then, the second brother married her and died and left no children, and then the third brother and so on until all seven brothers had married her and left no children. And lastly, the woman also died. The query that they presented to Jesus was: "At the resurrection, whose wife will she be?"

In Matthew's version of the gospel, Jesus answered: "You do err, not knowing the scriptures, nor the power of God. For in the resurrection, they neither marry, nor are given in marriage, but are as the angels of God in heaven" (22:29-30). Likewise Mark's Gospel states: "Do you not therefore err, because you know not the scriptures or the power of God? For when they shall arise from the dead, they neither marry, nor are given in marriage; but are as the angels which are in heaven" (12:24-25). Luke's version of Jesus' answer states: "And Jesus answering said unto them, the children of this world marry, and are given in marriage. But they which shall be accounted worthy to obtain that world, and the resurrection from the dead, neither marry or are given in marriage. Neither can they die any more, for they are equal unto the angels; and are the children of God, being the children of the resurrection" (Lk. 20:34-36). Therefore, all three gospels reflect that Jesus' answer states that the widow will not be the wife of any one of the seven brothers at the resurrection of the dead.

Moreover, Jesus says that there is no marriage, no sexual relationships, and no reproduction in heaven. In the resurrected life, we will all be God's children (sons and daughters). In like manner, death can no longer threaten the everlasting life of the resurrected. The gospel of Luke reports: "The dead are raised, when the Lord, the God of Abraham, and the God of Isaac, and the God of Jacob calls. For He is not a God of the dead, but of the living: for all live unto Him" (Lk. 20:37-38). In Jesus' perspective, the dead are related to God as well as to Abraham, Isaac, and Jacob. Hence in the New Testament, the dead are no longer gathered to their kin, but are carried by the angels to Abraham's bosom. This gives us great assurance to know that the spirit of those who die in Christ are carried immediately to heaven to be with Christ in Paradise. Further, Jesus accords the relationship with the Father and being in the presence of the Father as far more important than family ties and kindred relationships. According to Jesus Christ, the resurrection of believers refers to the individual's post-mortem exaltation to heaven.

In one of Jesus' parables, the story of "The Rich Man and Lazarus," we are able to appreciate His God-centered, anti-kinship perspective. The story goes that there was once a rich man who dressed in the finest apparel and feasted in great magnificence everyday. At his gate lay Lazarus who was covered with sores; he was a poor man and would have been glad to satisfy his hunger with the scraps from the rich man's table. When Lazarus died, he was carried by the angels into Abraham's bosom. The rich man also died and was buried and his soul was carried to a place of fire and torment. Looking up he saw, far away, Abraham with Lazarus at his side. He pleaded with Abraham to send Lazarus to dip the tip of his finger in water and cool his tongue. Abraham told him that this is not possible because "there is a great gulf fixed between us; no one from our side who wants to reach you can cross it, and no one may pass from your side to us" (Lk.16:22-24, 26). Then the rich man asked Abraham to send Lazarus to warn his five brothers so that they would not come to this place of torment. Likewise, Abraham was unable to send any one to warn his brothers of their impending fate if they did not follow God's commandments (Lk. 16:27-29). Moreover, the message of this parable is that the brothers should not wait for a warning from the grave because the dead cannot speak to the living. The living must listen to "Moses and the prophets," meaning the Word of God in the Scriptures.

Jesus' view on life after death did not include a concern for what happened to the dead body. Since the dead body is not the eternal part of the individual, Jesus comforts believers by saying, be not afraid of them that kill the body, but are not able to kill the soul (Matt.10:28; Lk.12:4). Furthermore, Jesus admonishes believers to "Take no though for your life, what you shall eat or what you shall drink, nor yet for your body, what you shall put on. Is not the life more than meat and the body more than raiment? But seek first the kingdom of God and His righteousness and all these things will be added unto you" (Matt.6:25,33; Lk.12:22,31). Whereas the body is essential for our earthly existence as a dwelling place; it is not necessary for eternal life. For the body without the spirit is dead (Ja.2:26). Moreover, when followers of Christ die their spirits go immediately to Paradise to be with Christ and the prophets.

Furthermore, when Jesus said to His disciples: "follow me." One said, Lord allow me to go first and bury my father. Jesus said to him: "Let the dead bury the dead, but you go and preach the kingdom of God" (Matt.8:21-22; Lk.9:59-60). And another also said, Lord I will follow you; but let me go first and say goodbye to those who are at my house. Moreover, Jesus said to him: "No man, having put his hand to the plough, and looking back, is fit for the kingdom of God" (Lk.9:61-62). Jesus' message and His entire focus was God-centered. Hence, our relationship with God through His Son Jesus Christ is the center of the Christian message. Therefore, Jesus did not focus much attention on what humans will find in heaven. What counts most is being in the presence of God the Father throughout all of eternity.

The relationship of the Father and Son can be summarized in one word "Abba," the Aramaic term for father. Biblically stated "Abba" refers to God as an exalted Father figure; however, for Christ it also denotes a relationship of intimacy and trust. Jesus considered this intimacy as uniquely special and He did not share it with anyone else. Moreover, Jesus serves as the intermediary between God and believers in Christ. Jesus says: "All things are delivered unto me of my Father, and no one knows the Son except the Father, and no one knows the Father except the Son and any one to whom the Son chooses to reveal to him" (Matt.11:27; Lk.10:22). For Jesus, heaven is not merely a place of material reward, but a place where believers can spend eternity in the presence of God the Father. Therefore, Jesus preached this message: "Any one who hears my Word and believes on Him that sent me has everlasting life and passes from death unto life" (Jn.5:24).

Likewise, Jesus' message to believers is to "Come unto me, all who labor and are heavy laden, and I will give you rest. Take my yoke upon you, and learn of me; for I am meek and lowly in heart, and you shall find rest unto your souls. For my yoke is easy and my burden is light" (Matt.11:28-29). To rest in God, now on this earth and later in heaven, means that you must focus on God alone, and not on worldly things. Rather, you must love God and have a personal and intimate relationship with Him through the Lord Jesus Christ. Therefore, you must "humble yourselves under the mighty hand of God, that he may exalt you in due time. Cast all your cares on Him for He cares for you" (I Pet.5:6-7). Hallelujah, "the God of all Grace has called us into His eternal glory by Christ. To Him be glory and dominion for ever and ever, A-men" (I Pet.5:10-11).

CHAPTER 16

PAUL'S SPIRITUAL BODIES

Synopsis

Chapter 16 explains Paul's concept of the "spiritual bodies." The contrast between the earthly corruptible body and the incorruptible body is clearly defined. In the final part of the chapter, the resurrection of the dead in Christ is discussed. Paul accepted the belief that when a person dies he "sleeps." Paul followed the tradition that delayed reunion with God to some future time. Paul's description of "spiritual bodies" is fully explained.

The Apostle Paul was a Pharisee who was converted on the road to Damascus and became a Christian (Acts 9:3-16). The Bible says that he immediately began his ministry as an apostle preaching that Jesus is the Son of God (Acts 9:20). Everything that Paul did and wrote was for the glory of God and the Lordship of Jesus Christ. Paul's perspective of life after death was based on a number of Jewish beliefs, including the notion that at death the person "sleeps." Like Jesus Christ, Paul forbade any form of ancestor worship, insisting that the resurrected Christ was the only person to be revered. However, in contrast to Christ who spoke in parables and told of believers joining Christ in Paradise immediately after death, Paul follows the Pharisaic tradition which delays the believers advent into heaven. He states that at an appointed time in the future, a resurrection of the dead shall occur (Acts 24:15). Moreover, Paul's perspective of eternal life is future oriented, rather than occurring presently. Paul writes: "As many of us as are baptized into Jesus Christ are baptized into His death. Therefore, just as Christ was raised up from the dead by the glory of the Father, even so we also should walk in the newness if life. For if we have been planted together in the likeness of His death, we shall be also in the likeness of His resurrection. Knowing this, that our old man is crucified with Him, that the body of sin might be destroyed. Now if we be dead with Christ, we believe that we shall also live with Him. For He died once to sin, but He lives unto God. Likewise, if we are dead to sin, we are alive to God through Jesus Christ our Lord" (Rom.6:3-11).

Paul states that the physical body (in contrast to the resurrected body) may be viewed as a temporary house where the ego, or soul, lives. According to Paul, God will prepare another home for our souls when death takes over this body. However, in order to move from our temporary home into our eternal home, we must die. Even Jesus had to die in order to shed His old body and take on a "resurrected body." Likewise, dead Christians must leave their physical bodies in the grave before they can move into their new home. Hence Paul states that God will eventually provide the dead with a new "spiritual body." Moreover, Paul writes: "So also is the resurrection of the dead. It is sown in corruption, it is raised in incorruption. It is sown in dishonor, it is raised in glory; it is sown in weakness, it is raised in power. It is sown a natural body, it is raised a spiritual body. For this corruptible must put on incorruptible, and this mortal must put on immortality. So when this corruptible shall have put on incorruptible, and this mortal shall have put on immortality, then shall be brought to pass the saying that is written, Death is swallowed up in victory" (I Cor.15:42-44, 53-54).

Although Paul did not state specifically what the "spiritual bodies" would be like, the Bible tells us that humans are made of two components. The first component is material and earthly and the second is spiritual and divine. In the first creation, God formed man from the dust of the ground, and breathed into his nostrils the breath of life and man became a living soul (Gen.2:7). However, at the resurrection, the new "spiritual body" will have no material parts. Hence, the new creation will be fully spiritual and immortal. The physical body will lie in the grave and go back to dust because it is no longer important.

Moreover, Paul writes: "The first man is of the earth, earthly; the second man is the Lord from heaven. And as we have borne the image of the earthly, we shall also bear the image of the heavenly" (I Cor. 15:47, 49). Furthermore, he states: "That I may know Him and the power of His resurrection, and the fellowship of His sufferings, being made conformable unto His death. If by any means I might attain unto the resurrection of the dead" (Phil.3:10-11).

Paul's "spiritual bodies" needed a new design and Paul intimates that the spiritual body would not have the anatomy and physiology of the earthly body because God would destroy both the stomach and the food in it. Therefore, Paul states that flesh and blood cannot inherit the Kingdom of God, neither does corruption inherit incorruption. Further, he says "I will show you a mystery, we shall not all sleep, but we shall all be changed. In a moment, in the twinkling of an eye, at the last trump, for the trumpet shall sound and the dead shall be raised incorruptible, and we shall be changed" (I Cor.15:50-52). Furthermore, Paul states: "But I would not have you to be ignorant concerning those who are asleep, that you sorrow not as those who have no hope. For if we believe that Jesus died and rose again, even so those that also sleep in Jesus will God bring with Him. And those of us who are alive and remain until the coming of the Lord, shall not prevent those who are asleep. For the Lord Himself shall descend from heaven with a shout, with the voice of the archangel, and with the trump of God, and the dead in Christ shall rise first. Then we who are alive and remain shall be caught up together with them in the clouds, to meet the Lord in the air, and so shall we ever be with the Lord. Wherefore comfort one another with these words" (I Thes. 4:13-18). And the very God of peace sanctify you wholly, and I pray God your whole spirit, soul and body be preserved blameless unto the coming of our Lord Jesus (I The. 5:23).

CHAPTER 17

JOHN'S HEAVENLY VISIONS

Synopsis

The final chapter of the book recounts the Apostle John's vision of heaven as recorded in the book of Revelation. In this report John recounts having experienced the same vision experience by the Old Testament prophet Ezekiel. Like the explanations of Jesus and Paul, John's visions reveal a God-centered heaven.

The Apostle John is the writer of the book of Revelation which he composed while he was exiled on the Isle of Patmos. Like the perspective of heaven as initially proposed by Jesus and expanded by Paul, John suggests that heaven is a place which is separate from this world and a place where believers find fulfillment in the presence of God. However, John's viewpoint of heaven differs from the perspectives of both Jesus and Paul in that he gives human form to God, the elders, the prophets, and the saints in heaven. Like other visionaries, John felt compelled to write down what he saw. Now realize that what John saw was deeply rooted in Jewish tradition. Therefore, John of Patmos re-lives and re-experiences the vision of Ezekiel, an Old Testament prophet who had lived some seven hundred years earlier.

Moreover, Ezekiel reports that while he was a captive by the river Che'-bar, the heavens were opened to him and he saw visions of God. Ezekiel describes seeing a person of a fiery nature, sitting on a throne and surrounded by four spirits with the likeness of a man. Every one had four faces and every one had four wings. As for the likeness of their faces, they each had the face of a man, the face of a lion, the face of an ox, and the face of an eagle (Ezek.1:1-10; 10:10). Whereas, earlier visionaries beheld God surrounded by angels or spirits, John perceived the throne of God surrounded by human forms as well.

In the first chapter of the book of Revelation, John calls the vision that God gave him, the Revelation of Jesus Christ and writes: "I was in the Spirit on the Lord's day, and heard behind me a great voice, as of a trumpet, saying, I am Alpha and Omega, the first and last, and what you see, write in a book and send it to the seven churches in Asia. And I turned to see the voice that spoke with me. I saw seven candlesticks and in the mist of the candlesticks, I saw one who looked like the Son of man, clothed with a garment down to the foot, and girt about with a golden girdle. His head and His hairs were white like wool, as white as snow; and His eyes were as a flame of fire. And His feet were like fine brass, as if they had burned in a furnace; and His voice sounded like many waters. And He had in His right hand seven stars, and out of His mouth went a sharp two-edged sword, and His countenance was as if the sun shined in His strength. And He laid His right hand upon me saying unto me, Fear not; I am the First and the Last: I am He that lives, and was dead; and behold, I am alive for evermore, A-men; and have the keys of hell and death. Write the things which you have seen, and the things which are, and the things which shall be hereafter" (Rev. 1:1-19). Moreover, John was to bear record of the Word of God and the testimony of Jesus Christ, and of all things which he saw.

John reports that he saw a door open in heaven, and he heard a voice say to him "Come up here, and I will show you things which must be hereafter." Entering the door John states that he is immediately in the spirit, and finds himself in heaven where he sees the divine throne and God sitting on the throne. The throne and the One who sat on the throne are so dazzling that their glorious appearance can only be described in terms of precious stones. Hence, John writes: "And He that sat on the throne looked like a jasper and sardine stone, and there was a rainbow around the throne the color of an emerald. And around the throne were four and twenty elders, clothed in white raiment with gold crowns on their heads. Out of the throne proceeded lightnings and thundering, and voices, and there were seven lamps of fire burning before the throne which are the seven spirits of God. And before the throne was a sea of glass like crystal, and in the midst of the throne, and round about the throne were four beasts full of eyes before and behind. The first beast looked like a lion, the second like a calf, and the third had a face like a man, and the fourth was like a flying eagle. And each of them had six wings, and were full of eyes. Day and night, they praised God saying, Holy! Holy! Holy! Lord God Almighty, which was, and is, and is to come. While God occupies His throne in heaven in awesome majesty; the spirits and the four and twenty elders give honor, thanks and worship to God, saying Thou are worthy, O Lord, to receive Glory and Honor and Power, for You have created all things, and for Your pleasure they are and were created (Rev. 4:1-11).

John reports that he saw in the right hand of Him that sat on the throne a book that was written within and sealed on the backside with seven seals. And a strong angel proclaims with a loud voice, who is worthy to open the book and loose the seals? And no one in heaven, or in the earth, or under the earth was able to open the book. John writes that he wept. And one of the elders told him to weep not: "Behold, the Lion of the tribe of Judah, the Root of David has opened the book and loosed the seals. And I saw in the midst of the throne and in the midst of the four and twenty elders, stood a Lamb that had been slain. And He came and took the book out of the hand of Him that sat on the throne. And when He had taken the book, the four beasts and the four and twenty elders fell down before the Lamb, each having harps, and golden vials full of the prayers of the saints." And they sang a new song, saying, "Thou art worthy to take the book, and to open the seals, for thou was slain, and has redeemed us to God by thy blood out of every kindred, and tongue, and people, and nation" (Rev.5:1- 9).

John proclaims that he saw a great multitude, which no man could number, of all nations, and kindreds, and peoples and tongues, standing before the throne, and before the Lamb. They were clothed in white robes and with palm branches in their hands. And they cried with a loud voice, saying, *"Salvation to our god which sitteth upon the throne, and unto the lamb."* All the angels, the elders, and the beasts bowed down and worshipped God by singing a new song and saying with a loud voice, Worthy is the Lamb that was slain, to receive power, and riches, and wisdom, and strength, and honor, and glory, and blessings, for ever and ever (Rev.7:9- 12)

The Bible says that one of the elders initiated a conversation with John and told him who these people were and why they were there:

> These are they which came out of great tribulation, and have washed their robes, and made them white in the blood of the Lamb. That is the reason why they stand before the throne of God, and serve Him day and night in his temple; and he who sits on the throne shall dwell with them. They shall never again feel hunger or thirst, the sun shall not beat on them nor any scorching heat. For the Lamb who is in the midst of the throne shall feed them, and shall lead them to the fountains of living water: and God shall wipe all tears from their eyes (Rev. 7).

Furthermore, John saw a great white throne and the dead small and great stood before God. And the books were opened, and another book, the book of life was opened, and the dead were judged by the things which were written in the books according to their works. And the sea gave up the dead which were in it; and death and hell delivered up the dead which were in them, and they each were judged according to their works. And whosoever was not found in the book of life was cast into the lake of fire (Rev.20:11-15). After the general resurrection of the dead, the Last Judgment ensures that any person whose name is not written in the book of life will be thrown into the burning lake. John proclaims that the others will be granted eternal life on a renewed earth.

Thus John writes: "And I saw a new heaven and a new earth: for the first heaven and the first earth was passed away; and there was no more sea. And I John saw the holy city, the new Jerusalem, coming down from God out of heaven, prepared as a bride adorned for her husband. And I heard a great voice out of heaven saying, Behold, the tabernacle of God is with men, and he will dwell with them, and they shall be his people, and God himself shall be with them, and be their God. And God shall wipe away all tears from their eyes; and there shall be no more death, neither sorrow, nor crying, neither shall there be any more pain, for the former things are passed away. And he that sat upon the throne said, Behold I make all things new. And he said unto me, It is done. I am Alpha and Omega, the beginning and the end. I will give unto him that is athirst of the fountain of the water of life freely. He that overcomes shall inherit all things; and I will be his God, and he shall be my son" (Rev.21:1-7).

While still in the spirit, John reports that one of the seven angels came to him and said: "Come up here and I will show you the bride, the Lamb's wife. And he carried me to a great and high mountain and showed me that great city, the holy Jerusalem, descending out of heaven from God. Having the glory of God and like a precious stone dazzling like jasper and clear as crystal" (Rev. 21:9-11). Moreover, John describes seeing heaven, which he calls the new and eternal Jerusalem descend from heaven and situate itself on earth.

The Apostle John describes the City of God, the New Jerusalem, as being a gigantic hall in the form of a cube with sides measuring about 1,500 miles. The construction of the tabernacle which John saw had a great and high wall and twelve gates, and at the gates twelve angels, and the names of the twelve tribes of Israel. John declares that he saw three gates on the east, three gates on the north, three gates on the south, and three gates on the west. And the wall of the city had twelve foundations, and in them the names of the twelve apostles of the Lamb. And the city is four square, and the length is as large as the breadth, and the city measures twelve thousand furlongs. The length and the breadth and the height of it are equal. The building of the wall of the new Jerusalem is of jasper, and the city was pure gold, like clear glass. And the twelve foundations of the wall of the city are each garnished with all manner of dazzling and precious stones. And the twelve gates are twelve different pearls, and the street of the city is pure gold as transparent as glass (Rev.21:12-21).

The twelve gates give access to heaven which is occupied by the dual throne of God and Christ (the Lamb). This Divine center radiates so much light that there is no need for the sun, or the moon to shine in it; for the Glory of God lightens it, and the Lamb is the light in it. And the nations of them which are saved shall walk in the light of it. And the gates of heaven shall not be shut because there is no night there. And nothing shall enter that defiles, works abomination or makes a lie. Only those whose names are written in the Lamb's book of life shall enter (Rev. 21:22-27).

In the closing chapter of Revelation John writes: "And he showed me a pure river of water of life, clear as crystal, proceeding out of the throne of God and of the Lamb ... and on either side of the river was the 'tree of life,' which bare twelve manner of fruits, and yielded her fruit every month, and the leaves of the tree were for the healing of the nations. And there shall be no more curse, but the throne of God and of the Lamb shall be in it; and his servants shall serve him. And they shall see his face, and his name shall be in their foreheads. And there shall be no night, or candle, neither light of the sun, for the Lord God gives them light and they shall reign for ever and ever" (Rev.22:1-5)

Therefore John declares that "These sayings are faithful and true, and the Lord God of the holy prophets sent his angel to show his servants what must shortly be done. 'Behold, I come quickly, blessed is he that keeps the sayings of the prophecy of this book.' And he said unto me, Seal not the sayings of the prophecy of this book, for the time is at hand. He that is unjust, let him be unjust still; and he which is filthy, let him be filthy still; and he that is righteous, let him be righteous still; and he that is holy, let him be holy still" (Rev. 22:6-11). Moreover, the Apostle John proclaims that Jesus said:

> And behold I come quickly; and my reward is with me, to give every man according as his works shall be. I am Alpha and Omega, the first and the last. I am the root and the offspring of David, and the bright and morning star. Surely I come quickly (vs.12, 13. 16, 20).

Hence, John closes the chapter with the following words: "Blessed are they that do his commandments, that they may have right to the tree of life, and may enter in through the gates of the city. And the Spirit and the bride say, Come. And let him that hears say, Come. And let him that is athirst come. And whosoever will, let him take the water of life freely. For I testify unto every man that hears the words of the prophecy of this book. If any man shall add unto these things, God shall add unto him the plagues that are written in this book. And if any man shall take away from the words of the book of this prophecy, God shall take away his part out of the book of life, and out of the holy city, and from the things that are written in this book. The grace of our Lord Jesus be with you all. A-men' (vs. 14, 17-19, 21).

BIBLIOGRAPHY

Attig, Thomas (1996). *How We Grieve*. New York: Oxford University Press, Inc.

Berry, Caroline (1987). *The Rights of Life: Christians and Bio-Medical Decision Making*. Toronto: Hodder & Sloughton Publishers.

Berkhof, Hendrikus (1964). *The Doctrine of the Holy Spirit*. Richmond: John Knox Press.

Blank, Jeanne (1998). *The Death of an Adult Child*. New York: Baywood Publishing Company.

Cooper, David. Man: *His Creation, Fall, Redemption, and Glorification*. Los Angeles: Biblical Research Society.

Corr, C. and Balk, D. (1996). *Handbook of Adolescent Death and Bereavement*. Springer Publishing Company.

Ferre', Nels (1951). *The Christian Understanding of God*. New York: Harper Brothers, Inc.

The Holy Bible: King James Version. (1990). U.S.A.: Thomas Nelson Publishers.

Pohle, Joseph (1944). *God: The Author of Nature and the Supernatural*. St. Louis: B. Herder Book Company.

Sawyers, Norma (1992). *A Personal Grief and a Reasonable Faith*. Dogwood Publishing.

Szasz, Thomas (1977). *The Theology of Medicine*. Baton Rouge: State University Press.

Van Iersel, B. et. al. (Eds.) (1979). *Heaven*. New York: The Seabury Press.

Nelson's New Illustrated Bible Dictionary. (1995). Nashville: Thomas Nelson Publishers.

INDEX

ABOUT THE AUTHOR

Dr. Lu Ethel Tate Green is a Licensed Minister, an Educational Psychologist and a Registered Nurse. She is a graduate of the Calvary Bible Institute in Washington, D.C. with a Diploma in Biblical Studies. In this book, Dr. Green relates her traumatic experience in the tragic death of her son in a motorcycle accident in April 1985 at 23 years of age. She shares how her personal encounter with Christ helped her not only to survive, but to overcome and become victorious in this situation. The death of her son led her to an in-depth study of God's Word in efforts to find answers to the questions of "where are You God?" and "why my son?" Dr. Green's searching of the Scriptures after her son's death was quite different from her previous study of the Bible. Her focus changed from a study that emanated from tradition to one that resulted from condition, that is, a searching to find herself and also to cope with what was happening in her life and family. Through prayer and the guidance of her late pastor, Dr. Green began an intense study of the Bible. In 1991, she was called by God to a ministry of evangelism and music. In 1995, she believes that God commissioned her to write a therapeutic Christian book about the death of her son and her grief. She wrote for two years accomplishing very little. In early 1998, God revealed to her that He did not want her to focus the book entirely on death, grief and mourning, He wanted her to write about life and eternal life, as well. God said that the message is not about Dr. Green and her son, Eric, but it is about Jesus Christ who suffered, bled, and died for us becoming a sacrifice for sin, and through His death, burial and resurrection, we have eternal life. Thus, the message being conveyed is the salvation of lost and dying souls.

Dr. Green received the Doctor of Philosophy Degree (Ph. D.) in Educational Psychology from Howard University in Washington, D.C. in August 1989 and completed a Post-Doctoral Research Fellowship in 1991. In the capacity of research fellow, she completed two important research studies related to minorities with disabilities and co-authored publications in the Journal of Rehabilitation, 60 (2), 28-32 and Rehabilitation Psychology, 39 (2), 113-121. She is the author of publications in the Journal of Negro Education, 59, 320-335 and the Encyclopedia of African-American Education, (1996), 181-184.

Dr. Green has had more than thirty years of extensive experience as a researcher, administrator and educator. In the capacity of Director of Research and Development at Howard University Hospital from 1977-1982, Dr. Green conducted research studies and published research reports pertaining to patient/family satisfaction with care and employee job satisfaction. She has an extensive science background in normal Anatomy and Physiology and Pathophysiology and possesses a Bachelor of Science Degree from Tuskegee University in Tuskegee, Alabama and a Master of Science Degree from The Catholic University of America in Washington, D.C. All of the above stated educational credentials and professional experiences qualify Dr. Green generally as a writer and specifically as a writer of a therapeutic Christian book concerning the phenomena of natural life, death, eternal life, bereavement and mourning.